He Heals
the Wounds of
Every Shattered Heart

Natasha Gray

ISBN 979-8-88943-602-7 (paperback)
ISBN 979-8-88943-603-4 (digital)

Christian Faith Publishing
832 Park Avenue
Meadville, PA 16335
www.christianfaithpublishing.com

Printed in the United States of America

To my niece, who was an inspiration to myself as well as many others. During her short time here on earth, she shined the light of Jesus in her life by way of her actions and her words. She is dearly missed by many.

I miss you every day, but I'm at peace knowing that you're with *your* Jesus in heaven, and one day I will see you again.

RIP, Baylei Marie M. (2/26/12–3/6/21).

Thank you also to all my amazing friends who have encouraged and supported me in the process of writing this book. I love you all so very much!

Contents

Introduction

He heals the wounds of every shattered heart.
—Psalm 147:3 (The Passion Translation)

Each one of us has a story, a tale to tell of how our hearts were shattered. For some, it was the loss of a relationship; for others, the loss of a loved one: a husband, wife, child, sibling, etc. Some people have watched their dreams shatter at their feet without knowing the causes of such harsh and brutal action. There are those whose hearts are shattered as a result of their actions or choices in life.

Whatever has caused your shattered heart, I want to tell you that there is hope. You may not feel this truth where you are located at the moment. You may feel that the darkness is too much to overcome. The pain you feel may seem like it's too great. The addiction may feel too strong.

On your own, yes, it can be incredibly difficult to walk through the darkness this world is shrouded in. You may feel weary, empty, pained, lost, or just plain done. I will tell you: There are times many of us have felt that way. There is hope, though! There is good news, and the good news is, you are not alone.

I don't know the reason you've picked up this book, but I want to prepare you for what you're about to read. Writing this book has been a lifelong dream that I honestly thought I wouldn't ever get to accomplish. It was the shaking of my faith by a loss I never saw coming that resulted in me digging my heels into my faith and making the decision to put my story to paper, the determination to use the testimony of not only my history but also those I have come into contact with over the years to inspire hope in those that feel just as lost as I once did.

There are going to be topics that are discussed that some people may not relate to, and that's okay! Praise God, you can't relate to everything in this book, but for the topics that you do, I wish I could wrap you up in a hug. This life can be difficult to navigate through, especially when our history is full of pain. It is possible to overcome the things that were once meant to break you.

My hope and prayer is that this book reaches that part of your heart, perhaps the part you've tried to hide away for fear of being judged, or perhaps it's been too painful to bring it to light. Maybe you've hidden it because you've had to rely on yourself instead of having people that you can rely on in your life. Whatever the reason for hiding that part of your heart is, I ask that you take a moment to take the deepest breath you can. Allow the walls to come down; allow God to come into that place and begin the healing process. I can't promise it will be easy, but it will be worth it.

1

My Story Begins: A Journey of Hope

We live in a fallen world; one only has to look out the window to see that. Trials happen to everyone every day. It doesn't matter how "good" of a person you are; trials will come. Sometimes, those trials feel like they may win. Too often, people sadly believe that if they're a "good enough" person, they won't have to go through the trials a "bad" person has to. That's not how this fallen world works, but I can promise you that if you allow God to be with you in those times of trial, you will come out stronger on the other side.

There will be times you will want to stop moving forward, times when the pain will feel too strong to overcome on your own. This is when it's vitally important to reach out to God. He will not only comfort you through the difficult time, but He will also give you the strength to press on. Where we are weak, God is strong.

> Concerning this I pleaded with the Lord three times that it might leave me; but He has said to me, "My grace is sufficient for you [My lovingkindness and My mercy are more than enough—always available—regardless of the situation]; for [My] power is being perfected [and is completed and shows itself most effectively] in [your] weakness." Therefore, I will all the more gladly boast in my weaknesses, so that the power

of Christ [may completely enfold me and] may
dwell in me. (2 Corinthians 12:8–9 AMP)

You may have a great relationship with God, and for that, I rejoice! You may not know who God is, or you may not have heard good things about God. If this is you, I ask that you open your heart to see who God truly is. Not through the eyes of religion, not through the experiences of those around you, but ask Him to show Himself to you. Ask Him, and He will reveal himself to you.

One thing I want you to understand is this: The fact that God isn't intimidated by our weaknesses, our failures, or our shortcomings. We are imperfect beings, but this doesn't scare Him. He isn't scared of the emotions we allow to overcome us. He is faithful, regardless of how our emotions fluctuate. There is a reason why the Bible states multiple times that He will never leave us nor forsake us.

One of the best things I have heard recently was this: Strong people have weak moments. Those weak moments do not define you. Wow. Read that again. Your weak moments don't define you. Your struggles don't define you. This may be the first time you're hearing this, and if it is, I pray that God touches your heart and shows you that your vulnerable, weak places do not scare Him; He wants to help you. He wants to connect with you. He wants to guide and help you. He wants to strengthen you by guiding you into a deeper relationship with Him.

One of the things I've learned over the years is that these things we see as weaknesses—temptations, addictions, struggles, lack of identity, and many other issues—all flourish in the darkness. If we keep them to ourselves, we don't risk people judging us for what we're currently going through or what we have gone through, but we also allow those things to fester, grow, and infect other areas of our life. This only increases the amount of pain we go through in the long run. It's similar to an infected cut. If it's treated early on, even when it's painful, it won't be given the chance to grow worse and cause more damage. The choice is yours. It's better to address these things while they're still small rather than try to uproot a longtime problem. I have had to learn this lesson in my own life many times over the years.

One of the most powerful things to remember is that our testimony could also be the turning point for someone else who feels just as alone as we did when we were in the midst of our valley—whether that be an addiction, loss, or something else the world has thrown our way. Sharing our story will not only bring light to the place where those issues flourish, bringing healing along with it, but it also brings light to those who are going through similar struggles and feeling alone. It's amazing just how God can use our testimony, our painful experiences, to offer hope to those who are still walking through the darkness. You have to be open to allow God to use those areas that you may have found shameful at one point—or perhaps still do. This may take time, and that's okay. Take the first step and recognize the issue; bring it to light even if it's just you realizing that there is an issue.

By bringing these issues to light, you not only rob them of their power over you, but you also allow healing from God as well. This is when a test can become a testimony. Once you cut the vine off from the root, the vine dies. It may not be immediate, but it does die off. Are you willing to cut the vine? The vine of addiction. The vine of shame, of guilt. Perhaps the vine is lies you've been told and believed, but you want to change that.

It may be a one-time decision for some, but for others, it may end up being a daily decision. Even if this has to be a daily decision for you, *do it*. The first step may be the hardest, but with time, each step becomes a little easier than the last.

The purpose of this book is this: To be the book I wish I'd had when I was in my youth. When I was lost, scared, and unsure where to turn for help and I wished I had something like this available to me. To know that there was hope in the darkness I found myself wrapped up in. To know there was a way out.

There is hope and light in the darkness; you just have to look for it.

I'll be open and honest with you: It has not been easy being open about some of my history in the process of creating this book. There have been times, while writing, when I asked God if I should include particular parts of my story. Each time He reminded me that someone else may be struggling the same way I did and need to know they're not alone. So this is a sign to whoever needed to see it: You are not alone.

Let me start where my testimony began: Around the age of five, I was living in an apartment building with my mom, my stepdad, and my baby sister. In this apartment building, there was a play area enclosed by the buildings, giving children room to play and making it easy for the parents to keep an eye on their kids as they played. I often played there as it was just a few yards from my apartment. I enjoyed being able to play on the play structure with the other children that lived in the apartment building.

It was on this playground that I was first exposed to sex. I was told to keep it a secret as it was a "game," so I agreed to do so without questioning it. Someone older than me wanted to play with me; I wasn't about to risk losing that because I told someone else about a game we were playing. I didn't see the harm in keeping the secret at the time.

Being exposed to sex at such an innocent age altered my life forever. I didn't think anything of the secrecy; it was just something friends did. I didn't think what was happening was wrong. I was too young to understand what was going on and that it was a form of sexual abuse. This continued for a few years until those boys ended up moving away. When they left, I was left with confusion about what was normal in a friendship—especially between a girl and a boy—and what wasn't. I didn't feel that I could talk to my parents about what was going on as I had kept it secret for so long. This was the feeling of shame, but I didn't know what shame was at that time. I was left to adjust to this change in my life with many questions, but I had no way to get answers. This was where my addiction began.

Having been exposed to such an intimate act at such a young age, my understanding of what sex's proper role was in a healthy relationship was skewed. I thought it was something fun to do; I was focused on what I got out of the act and, as such, didn't concern myself with the partner I was supposed to be with. I didn't understand it as the intimate act that it is.

This seed of addiction stayed buried in the darkness of my silence about the events that occurred. It wouldn't sprout until many years later, but during that time, the devil planted roots that dug deeper into the darkness. I knew something about the whole thing was wrong, but I couldn't place my finger on it. Perhaps it was because of the secrecy involved among all the children. It wasn't until a few years later when I was attending church with my mom that I understood the gravity of what happened, but once again, my understanding would be altered in a way that would lead me deeper into the darkness rather than set me free.

I remember sitting in the church with my mom. I don't remember why I wasn't in the children's church that day, but I remember sitting next to her when the pastor was speaking. He spoke of how sex before marriage was a sin, and that God hated sin. I remember feeling my heart drop in my chest the moment I heard that. I'm sure there was more that he spoke about, but with the immediate guilt I felt over what had happened all those years ago, I felt lost as to what to do from then on. Cue the devil whispering into my young ear. If God hated sin, then how would my parents feel about what had happened to me? I had allowed it to happen. I couldn't tell my parents. The last thing I wanted was for them to confirm that what I had done was a sin, and since God hated sin, God hated me. This misunderstanding only pulled me farther away from the church and God.

My mom would read stories about Jesus and tell me about how He died on the cross for us, but I never truly believed that He died for me, thinking my sin was too much for Him. I didn't understand grace or mercy. I didn't feel that I deserved it. It was around this time that I began to struggle with the idea of others not having struggles like my own. I thought that God's love was for *them* but not for me. I had done too much for God to forgive me.

I don't recall why we stopped going to that particular church. My grandmother would take me to her church now and again when I got to spend time with her, and I enjoyed her church even though I still struggled with the confusion of God and His mercy.

A few years back, my grandmother sent me a card I'd written on while in church with her when I was around nine. On the card read: "Shut up, you stupid devil, I'm going to heaven." I recall being conflicted when the children's church talked about how we would go to heaven when we accepted Jesus as our Savior. When I wasn't at church, the devil would argue with me that I wasn't going to be allowed into heaven because I had screwed up too much for God to use me.

It wasn't until my seventh grade year that I would go to church again without someone from my family beside me. A friend of mine had invited me to her church as she was performing in an Easter play with her sister and wanted me to be there. While I had felt that tug of guilt about going, I still thought God hated me; I wanted to support her, so I said yes.

Her church was about a ten-minute walk away from where I lived with my family, so I decided to walk there alone. The entire walk there, I felt as if something was pulling, pushing at me not to go, trying to keep me from walking into that church building. The urge to support my friend was greater, though; I wanted to be there for her.

Once I arrived, I moved to the front row of the sanctuary. I recall sitting close to the aisle, thinking that if I needed to leave quickly, I'd have an easier time without anyone blocking my ability to do so. Even while sitting in the pew, waiting for the service to begin, I could hear a voice in the back of my head telling me that I wasn't wanted there, that God hated me, and that He was furious that I dare step foot into His house. I had to fight those thoughts and forced myself to sit there. I'd made a promise, and I planned on keeping it.

It wasn't long before my friend and her sister made their way out, and the play began. Little by little, that voice in the back of my head began to die off. I began to feel a warmth replacing it as I sat there, listening to what the pastor was saying about Jesus. I remember him speaking about how Jesus died on the cross for us, for each and every person, no matter their sin. That through Jesus, there was forgiveness; there was hope. This was the first time in a long time that I'd felt any sense of hope. While I had heard people talk about Jesus and how much he loved us, how his sacrifice on the cross saved us, this was the first time it began to sink in deep and uproot the lies I had believed for so long—lies that had kept me bound in darkness.

Sitting there, I had a choice: to allow God in and allow Him into the darkest parts of myself or to run back to that darkness that was so familiar. I chose to let God in. There were still parts of my life I wasn't fully ready to give Him, but I asked for Jesus to be my savior, and I asked for Him to forgive me for all that I'd done. I knew that I couldn't live in that darkness any longer. There was still much that I had to learn, but this was the beginning of the transformation in my life.

I had felt like I was locked in a dark, musky room for so long, and in that moment in that church, the door was opened; Jesus's light shone in and showed me there was a better way. I just had to reach out to Him and accept His help. He wouldn't force me to accept His help; it was my choice. It would have been so easy to refuse to move from the darkness that I had known for so long, to stay with what felt comfortable and familiar. While the darkness was known, the other aspects of it were also pain, loss, and confusion. While I didn't know what to expect from God, it had to be better than the pain the darkness offered.

> So you have not received a spirit that makes you fearful slaves. Instead, you received God's Spirit when he adopted you as his own children. Now we call him, "Abba Father." (Romans 8:15 NLT)

> So now there is no condemnation for those who belong to Christ Jesus. (Romans 8:1 NLT)

> I am convinced that nothing can ever separate us from God's love. Neither death nor life, neither angels nor demons, neither our fears for today nor our worries about tomorrow, not even the powers of hell can separate us from God's love. No power in the sky above or in the earth

> below-indeed, nothing in all creation will ever
> be able to separate us from the love of God that
> is revealed in Christ Jesus our Lord. (Romans
> 8:38–39 NLT)

This last scripture was the one I held onto during the darkest of times during my transition from the darkness into the light. The assurance that no matter how bad things got, God's love was strong enough to overcome it was something I clung to. The fact that His love for me was unconditional gave me hope I hadn't felt in a long time. A weight had been lifted. I felt like I could breathe—truly breathe.

Everyone has something in their life that they feel is a mountain that is impossible to climb. Whether it be an addiction, a mental struggle such as depression, a physical ailment, our circumstances in our lives or in the lives of those around us. The issue that many of us face when attempting to overcome these mountains is that we try to do it by our own abilities, our own strength. Instead of inviting God into these difficult areas, we feel that we have to overcome them before we can go to God.

There is a false belief that we have to meet some imaginary or unattainable standard before we can make our way to God. This can severely inhibit our growth as Christians. We can get to the point where we believe that we need to prove ourselves worthy to God before we can ask Him for help. Believing this only draws us deeper into the darkness and away from God.

> God saved you by his grace when you
> believed. And you can't take credit for this; it is
> a gift from God. Salvation is not a reward for
> the good things we have done, so none of us can
> boast about it. (Ephesians 2:8–9 NLT)

Salvation is a gift given by God to us. We don't have to meet a certain standard in order to receive salvation. It is offered to the gang member, the murderer, the drug addict, the drug dealer, the prostitute, just as it is offered to the single mom, single dad, CEO of a business, politician, and teacher. You don't have to have your life together in order to be accepted or used by God. God can use our brokenness in ways that we could never expect or imagine.

> Jesus returned to the Mount of Olives, but early the next morning he was back again at the Temple. A crowd soon gathered, and he sat down and taught them. As he was speaking, the teachers of religious law and the Pharisees brought a woman who had been caught in the act of adultery. They put her in front of the crowd. "Teacher," they said to Jesus, "this woman was caught in the act of adultery. The law of Moses says to stone her. What do you say?" They were trying to trap him into saying something that they could use against him, but Jesus stooped down and wrote in the dust with his finger. They kept demanding an answer, so he stood up again and said, "All right, but let the one who has never sinned throw the first stone!" Then he stooped down again and wrote in the dust. When the accusers heard this, they slipped away one by one, beginning with the oldest, until only Jesus was left in the middle of the crowd with the woman. Then Jesus stood up again and said to the woman, "Where are your accusers? Didn't even one of them condemn you?" "No, Lord." She said. And Jesus said, "Neither do I. Go and sin no more." (John 8:1–11 NLT)

One of the main things I want to point out with this scripture is when the people focused on religion—the law of Moses—they were quick to point out the sin and punishment for such in others. Jesus, however, saw through their religious attitude right to their heart. He didn't say, "Let the one who has never committed adultery throw the first stone." He said, "Let the one who has never sinned throw the first stone."

He didn't deny nor defend what this woman had done. All He did was turn their judgmental, pointing fingers at themselves. They were forced to admit in public that they were not as sinless as they wanted others to believe.

This had to be a major blow to their egos. To be a religious leader back in the days of Jesus is similar to being a celebrity in the modern day.

While they may have had the education to know what the law was, they did not have a heart for people. Their actions proved this as they used this woman in an attempt to trip up Jesus. They wanted Him to say something that they could use against Him because He challenged their way of life, the way things had been done for centuries. They were content with their power, their level of respect from the public. They didn't want to give that up and often challenged Jesus, trying to find ways to trick him, but every time, Jesus showed compassion to those that were being used with malicious intent, showing the true color of the Pharisees.

The Pharisees' actions or accomplishments in life didn't affect Jesus as they would the other people of that time. Where "normal" townsfolk would stand in awe at these leaders, Jesus saw past all the glitz, glamor, and puffed-up pride to see the dark hearts they had inside. They didn't care if the woman lived or died as long as they got what they wanted. Jesus called them out on it and publicly shamed them while reminding the people watching that these leaders weren't as sinless as they claimed to be. It's dangerous to allow yourself to be more focused on the law than on the one who created the law to begin with.

Let's shift gears and focus on how Jesus treated the woman brought to him. Women back in Jesus's time weren't treated well. They were often treated quite badly, and Jesus knew this. This was part of the reason behind the leaders bringing her to Jesus saying she was to be stoned. They didn't care about the woman for who she was; all they saw was what she had been caught doing.

Since this woman was caught in the act, I highly doubt they waited for her to put her clothes back on and look presentable before she was brought to Jesus. She may not have been allowed or able to grab anything to cover herself and was most likely humiliated, standing there not only in front of Jesus but also in front of the crowd that he had been teaching. The only thing she could do in her mind was wait for her death sentence to be carried out.

Jesus didn't lift a finger toward her, though. He didn't speak harshly toward her for her actions, nor did He even ask her if she was guilty of the crime she'd been accused of. Jesus treated her with compassion. He didn't condemn her; He didn't tell her she only had two more chances at being forgiven before He was done doing so. He showed her respect, love, and compassion. I could only imagine her surprise when she heard Jesus telling the leaders of the time that they didn't have a leg to stand on! Most likely, no one saw this coming.

"Neither do I. Go and sin no more." I want to make a quick little note here: Jesus was not asking her to be perfect from then on out. He was encouraging her that she was to be free from the sinful lifestyle that she'd been living in. He gave her hope for a better life after this experience. If this woman—or any of us for that matter—could live a life without sin, why would Jesus need to sacrifice himself on the cross?

So often, we can define ourselves by our experiences. We carry them on our backs as burdens or wear them around our necks with pride. Both can be dangerous. Our experiences do not define who we are in God's eyes. His love for us goes much deeper. So much so that He knows intimately the emotions we go through with trials.

Jesus dealt with loss, betrayal, rejection; and He suffered in ways most of us could never understand in order for us to have a way to reconnect with God. Because of Jesus, we are able to have an intimate relationship with God. We can know Him as a friend, as a provider, as a healer, a counselor, a father. I will go more in-depth with this topic in a later chapter. We don't have to have our heads bowed to the ground because of what we've been through. Through Jesus, our past has lost its ability to define us.

On the other hand, if we carry our experiences around our neck with pride, we can begin to rely on our own strengths and abilities to overcome instead of rely on God and His provision. This can hinder our growth not only as Christians but also as people. When we become self-reliant, we are less likely to listen to those who guide us with advice, those that only want to help us stay on the right path. This pride puts a strain on not only our relationship with other people but with God as well. If we are closed off to hearing what others have to say, we could lose the chance to hear something that God is trying to speak to us through someone else. This can become a stumbling block in our lives if we do not address such an issue head-on.

> Fear of the Lord is the foundation of true knowledge, but fools despise wisdom and discipline. (Proverbs 1:7 NLT)

I want to clarify something: "Fear" of the Lord isn't about being scared of Him in the way some interpret it. God does not want us to be scared to approach Him. We may disappoint Him due to our failures; however, when we acknowledge what we did was wrong, admit our shortcomings to Him, then our connection is strengthened. Fear of the Lord means to have reverent respect for Him. It means to recognize that God is greater than anything of this world; it is to be in awe of Him.

There are times that the devil will try to trip Christians up by twisting the words used in the Bible, but we must remember to keep them in context, and if we're confused about how something is worded, we need to be willing to speak to someone who may have more information on the subject such as a pastor, a teacher, or a mentor.

The Amplified Bible puts this verse another way:

> The [reverent] fear of the Lord [that is, worshiping Him and regarding Him as truly awesome] is the beginning and the preeminent part of knowledge [its starting point and its essence];
> But arrogant fools despise [skillful and godly] wisdom and instruction and self-discipline.

There is a reason that pride comes before a fall. When we walk in pride, we put ourselves above or below others in our own category. Pride isn't always about strutting around, thinking you're better than anyone else with your nose up in the air. It's also thinking that you're in a category that no one else can reach or understand. Pride puts the self first, and that will always end with that person falling flat on their face at some point or another. Our circumstances can change in an instant, and pride can hinder your ability to handle the shift.

Proverbs 13:20 (NLT) warns: "Walk with the wise and become wise; associate with fools and get in trouble. You can overcome pride by returning God to his rightful place as first in your life."

> "My thoughts are nothing like your thoughts," says the Lord. "And my ways are far beyond anything you could imagine. For just as the heavens are higher than the earth, so my ways are higher than your ways and my thoughts higher than your thoughts." (Isaiah 55:8–9 NLT)

Let me fill you in on a little secret: we will never know everything about God. He is the one that created each and every person from Adam and Eve to the last human that is to be born. He created the mountains and the seas. Every living creature, He created it all with a purpose—though there are a few I question His reasoning on. (Looking at you, wasps, mosquitoes, and fleas!)

God created you with a purpose as well. Sometimes the path to getting there is full of twists and turns, bumps, potholes, mountains, and valleys. It will be worth it when you get to the destination God has for you. Don't allow your circumstances, your history, to hinder your belief that God has amazing plans for your life—including all those circumstances.

> Trust in the Lord with all your heart; do not depend on your own understanding. Seek his will in all you do, and he will show you which path to take. (Proverbs 3:5–6 NLT)

Take a moment and ask God to help make your path straight. Sometimes, we get so focused on how *we* want life to go that we forget that God is supposed to be guiding *us*. How often has life gone your way? Give Him back the wheel and trust in Him. He loves *you*.

> A man's mind plans his way [as he journeys through life], But the Lord directs his steps and establishes them. (Proverbs 16:9 AMP)

2

Trials: God Is with You

Even when I walk through the darkest valley I will
not be afraid for you are close beside me. Your rod
and your staff protect and comfort me.

—Psalm 23:4 (NLT)

Read that scripture again. Take a moment and think about what it means. The scripture above does not say that we camp out in the darkest valley. What's your dark valley? Addiction? Promiscuity? Drinking? Smoking? Loss? Self-harm? Whatever that dark valley is, address it.

The first step to winning the battle is recognizing what it is we're fighting against. If your darkest valley is addiction, write down what that addiction is to. Write down what may have led to that being an addiction in your life. That goes for any of the other issues. What led to you participating in promiscuity? What led to excess drinking? What pain has led you into thinking of self-harm as a way to cope? Don't judge yourself when you're writing these down. Your pain is just as real as the pain of anyone else.

Everyone has some area of their life that they're weak in. There's no shame in that as it's a part of being a human. As I mentioned in the last chapter, by bringing to light what it is that you're struggling with, you are pulling it out of the darkness and refusing to give it a place to hide and fester any more.

We don't set up residence in the dark valley and make that darkness our home. If that darkness has been your home for a long time, make the choice to change. Make the choice to no longer live in that darkness but allow God to help lift you up and move forward. The enemy will fight to attempt to keep you in the dark, but if you want to be free. you have to make the decision to change. God will be with you. Just like He said he would be in Psalm 23:4 (NLT): "Even when I walk through the darkest valley, I will not be afraid, for you are close beside me. Your rod and your staff protect and comfort me."

The steps (1) addressing the issue, (2) stating what led to the issue, (3) realizing you need help are steps in the right direction. The next step is clear in the scripture above: We walk through that dark valley with God. That valley may be long, but there is a light at the end of it, there is hope.

Walking through something is a choice that only you can make. No one can force your hand. No one can force you to address the issues in your life. There will be those that can encourage and support you along the road, but ultimately, you must be willing to do the work. Having a support system is vital when it comes to walking through a dark valley.

I've found that it's in this valley that the devil enjoys attacking the most. This is in part because it is when we are the most vulnerable. It's when we may be or feel alone, isolated, overwhelmed, or lost. The fear of judgment from either God or others can keep us rooted in that valley and sap any and all hope that we have of ever getting out. This is why it's so vital to bring this valley to the light with someone you trust.

This person could be your family, your friends, your coworker, or a member of your church. I can say that my church family has been the best help when it came to dealing with dark valleys in my life. There were things I wasn't ready or willing to discuss with my family due to fear of how they would see me, how I would be treated if I spoke to them about some of the issues I was dealing with, but people in my church offered unwavering support and encouragement. Part of their assistance was sharing their stories with me about their dark valleys and how God brought them through it. Knowing that someone else has been through a similar valley and is ready and willing to walk with you as you walk through your own offers hope.

It can be easy to fall into self-reliance when difficult times come for a few reasons. One of the main ones being fear of how others will view us. We get more concerned with the image we hold than we are concerned with getting through the valley.

Aside from fear, another reason is someone hasn't had deep meaningful connections with other people. This could be a lack of family connection or a lack of friends while in a vulnerable age. Also, they may have been let down by the people they thought would stay with them through a valley before. This lack of connection in our life can build up the lie that no one else will be there for us, so we need to be there for ourselves and rely only on ourselves. This can cause serious trust issues, which only deepens the immediate problem and also cause others down the road.

One of the best ways to address these connection issues is the same as addressing what led to the dark valley you may be in. What happened in your history to cause these types of behaviors—the self-isolation, the disconnect from others, what boundaries have you allow to be crossed instead of enforcing them. Again, don't judge yourself, but be honest in your assessment. This is the only way that you can truly find the root of the problem by facing them head-on.

Asking God to help you identify what caused the disconnection is one step that will help in your journey out of the valley. There will be times when life simply throws you a curveball and you end up in a dark valley, such as an unexpected loss of a loved one or the loss of a job. Not all the time is it our actions or inactions that lead to the valley. In this fallen world, valleys are a part of life for everyone. Being prepared with God's help can help you through them when they do come and you can come out stronger on the other side.

Notice the Scripture didn't say we run or skip through the valley either. We can get so focused on the destination that we learn nothing during the journey.

This type of mindset—focusing on the end result—doesn't help our testimony nor does it help our individual growth. Our testimony is one of the most powerful tools we have. We can use our testimony to reach out to others that are going through similar situations and offer them guidance, hope, comfort, and even walk alongside them through their valley.

We also have the potential to learn through the situations that we go through. We have the opportunity to learn what's most important to us, and sometimes, we learn more about ourselves than if we hadn't gone through the valley in the first place. Sometimes, I'm reminded that what the enemy meant for evil, God will turn around for His good.

> As for you, you meant evil against me, but God meant it for good in order to bring about this present outcome, that many people would be kept alive [as they are this day]. (Genesis 50:20 AMP)

This journey of life starts with faith. We won't know the end result before we start. When in life do we know how something will end before we begin? Even when we're born, we don't know the road our life will go down. When we have a child, we don't know how they will end up as they grow up. When we begin a new job, we have no idea how long we will stay there or if we will be called to a different line of work. Life requires faith and taking steps into an unknown future.

There will be times we will make mistakes. Some choices we make we will find out later on in life were choices we shouldn't have made. All that can be used by God if we allow Him to. God can use the mistakes we've made in our life to shape us into the people He created us to be. Nothing is impossible for Him. No situation is too hopeless for Him to use it for His glory.

Another part of the scripture above I want to focus on is the fact that we do not walk in the darkness alone. *"For you are close beside me."* God isn't watching from afar waiting to see how you handle this time alone—no! He is right there with you, walking through the pain and uncertainty. There will be times you wonder if He is there.

You may feel alone, lost, confused. Even through all this, there is hope. He promises in His word never to leave us nor forsake us.

> Be strong and courageous, do not be afraid
> or tremble in dread before them, for it is the Lord
> your God who goes with you. He will not fail
> you or abandon you. (Deuteronomy 31:6 ESV)

God is good even when the situations in life are not. He is with us even when we feel alone; we need only to call on Him, and He will guide us. There's a saying that the teacher is always quiet during the test. I can't explain why some people feel God is with them when they call out and others don't. I don't know, but I do know that God is still good, that He promised to be by our side, and we can't go by what we feel when it comes to our faith. Our faith has to be in Him and Him alone no matter what circumstances are thrown our way. His word is our guide when the road gets tough.

> I have told you all this so that you may have
> peace in me. Here on earth you will have many
> trials and sorrows. But take heart, because I have
> overcome the world. (John 16:33 NLT)

The Passion Translation says it this way: "And everything I've taught you is so that the peace which is in me will be in you and will give you great confidence as you rest in me. For in this unbelieving world you will experience trouble and sorrows, but you must be courageous, for I have conquered the world!"

We have a choice to rest in God and His promises. This scripture was spoken by Jesus to encourage us to hold tight to our faith in Him. This world will throw trials and tribulations our way, and the enemy will do anything to make us stumble, especially when we're striving to live with God's Word as our guide in life. One important thing to remember is what society says is acceptable, appropriate, or approved isn't the same thing as what God says is.

What sorrow for those who say that evil is good and good is evil, that dark is light and light is dark, that bitter is sweet and sweet is bitter. (Isaiah 5:20 NLT)

All Scripture is inspired by God and is useful to teach us what is true and to make us realize what is wrong in our lives. It corrects us when we are wrong and teaches us to do what is right. (2 Timothy 3:16 NLT)

Expect to be hated by all because of my name, but be faithful to the end and you will experience life and deliverance. (Matthew 10:22 TPT)

"Listen to my words," Jesus said. "Anyone who leaves his home behind and chooses me over children, parents, family, and possessions, all for the sake of the gospel, it will come back to him a hundred times as much in this life-time-homes, family, mothers, brothers, sisters, children, possessions-along with persecutions. And in the age to come he will inherit eternal life. But many who are considered to be the most important now will be the least important then. And many who are viewed as the least important now will be considered the most important then." (Mark 10:29–31 TPT)

The meaning behind the last verse confused me for some time. Once I became more mature in the faith, I began to understand that in our lives, there will be people that we love that won't want to serve God. We will have to make a choice between staying with our family members, staying friends with people that may not want to worship God or don't support us in going where God has called us to be. Standing on the Word of God will definitely not sit well with some people, but we are not called to please people. We are called to please God. This can be difficult when those you care about abandon you because you choose God over them.

We must, however, put our relationship with God above all others.

He must be our foundation or we will surely fall.

> So everyone who hears these words of Mine and acts on them, will be like a wise man [a far-sighted, practical, and sensible man] who built his house on the rock. And the rain fell, and the floods and torrents came, and the winds blew and slammed against that house; yet it did not fall, because it had been founded on the rock. And everyone who hears these words of Mine and does not do them, will be like a foolish (stupid) man who built his house on the sand. And the rain fell, and the floods and torrents came, and the winds blew and slammed against that house; and it fell—and great and complete was its fall. (Matthew 7:24–27 AMP)

The best thing you can do in this instance is to pray for those in your life, but choose God first. This isn't always easy. As a Christian, I have lost friendships that I thought would last a lifetime because I chose to draw closer to God. I had friends that would try to hold me back from growing closer to God. It was never an outwardly spoken comment in such, but they would become offended when I would grow and start to question my motives for growth.

There was one person I'd known for years. During an argument, she commented on my reasoning for trying to grow closer to God and be a better Christian, claiming it was a show for people at our church. It had hurt when this happened, but I knew that I wanted to grow closer to God, and if that meant letting go of that friendship, then so be it. I had to grieve over the lost friendship not only with this person but also with many others who chose to walk away once my friendship with that person dissolved.

Your relationship with God will be the most important in your life. Others will come and go; even family falls into this category at times, but God will *always* be with you.

Jesus knew that we would have trials and sorrows in our life, but we have a choice. We can choose to let those things keep us down, trap us as their prisoner, or we have a choice to accept the peace that Jesus offers us and rest in Him. This doesn't mean that we decide to just sit down and take the trials as they come; we have to walk through them like I mentioned before. We accept the situation we're in but walk forward and use that situation to push us toward God instead of away from Him. We walk in faith. We walk believing that God is going to bring us through and we will come out stronger on the other side.

> The LORD himself goes before you and will be with you; he will never leave you nor forsake you. Do not be afraid; do not be discouraged. (Deuteronomy 31:8 NIV)

The Lord will never leave us. To know without a doubt that no matter how bad the pain hurts we are not alone is such a reassurance! No matter how dark the night may seem to be, there is a light right beside you. There is hope no matter how hopeless the situation may appear. God makes a way when there seems to be no way. He did this over and over again in the Old Testament with His people.

> I am the Lord, who opened a way through the waters, making a dry path through the sea. (Isaiah 43:16 NLT)

God is with us always, but we also have to be aware that the enemy will stop at nothing to keep us from fulfilling the plans and purposes God has for our lives. One of the tactics the enemy likes to try to hinder us is lies. The enemy tries to get us to believe is that our situation is unique to us, that no one else will be able to understand the emotions that we're going through. This can cause us to be hostile when another person attempts to help by coming alongside us. He knows that if he can isolate us away from other Christians, he's able to make us his playground.

If he can make us believe that we've missed something as Christians, that other Christians don't struggle with what we're struggling with, we won't turn to them for help. We will pull ourselves away for fear of judgment, rejection, or simply the fear of disappointing someone we look up to. Once he's able to accomplish this, it's then that he starts to pressure us to question our salvation. The enemy wants us stopped so we don't reach others for God.

> The thief's purpose is to steal and kill and destroy. My purpose is to give them a rich and satisfying life. (John 10:10 NTL)

The Passion Translation reads, "But I have come to give you everything in abundance, more than you expect-life in its fullness until you overflow." The enemy wants you weak; he wants you blaming yourself, your actions or inactions, or even God for the hardships you've endured. He wants to shift the blame off him as this will prevent you from going to God and allowing Him to help you through the difficulties that life throws your way.

The devil is sneaky when he does this. He doesn't run around in a red suit with a pitchfork. At times, he will speak through friends that mean well but end up causing more harm than good. He'll speak through family members that are supposed to be supporting and encouraging you. He will find your weak points and aim shots directly at them. He knows if he can take you away from your stronghold, your shelter, your relationship with God, then he's able to make you ineffective for God's kingdom and in doing so further his own.

> When doubt filled my mind, your comfort gave me renewed hope and cheer. (Psalm 94:19 NLT)

> He comforts us in all our troubles so that we
> can comfort others. When they are troubled, we
> will be able to give them the same comfort God
> has given us. (2 Corinthians 1:4 NLT)

God knows your specific situation intimately. He knows the pain you are going through. Loss, grief, anger, doubt—all of it He knows and understands. I want to make one thing clear: God does not cause bad things to happen. Bad things happen because we live in a fallen world. The devil is in charge of this world. This happened the moment Adam and Eve sinned. Adam had been given authority by God over the world, but he gave it to the devil when he and Eve ate the forbidden fruit. (The good news is that Jesus took the keys back when He rose from the grave).

> Next the devil took him to the peak of a very
> high mountain and showed him all the kingdoms
> of the world and their glory. "I will give it all to
> you," He said "if you will kneel down and wor-
> ship me." (Matthew 4:8–9 NLT)

This was when Jesus was being tempted in the wilderness. If this was an empty promise, it wouldn't have been a real temptation. John 12:31 (NLT) reads, "The time for judging this world has come, when satan, the ruler of this world, will be cast out."

> Satan, who is the god of this world, has
> blinded the minds of those who do not believe.
> They are unable to see the glorious light of the
> Good News. They don't understand this message
> about the glory of Christ, who is the exact like-
> ness of God. (2 Corinthians 4:4 NLT)

"Has blinded the minds of those who do not believe." This is a very important part of that scripture. The enemy wants to steal our belief

in God. If he can do that, then we will be blinded by him and unable to be of use to God.

If we believe that God is to blame for our difficult circumstances in life, then we won't go to Him when we need reassurance, support, comfort, guidance, hope, or peace. We will turn to the things of this world and hope that it fills the void in our hearts. Nothing in this world—no relationship, no job, no amount of money, no house, no amount of kids, no amount of material things, nothing in this world can satisfy the God-sized hole in our heart, in our spirit. That can only be filled by God.

> Don't copy the behavior and customs of this world, but let God transform you into a new person by changing the way you think. Then you will learn to know God's will for you, which is good and pleasing and perfect. (Romans 12:2 NLT)

It can be so tempting—especially at a young age, an impressionable age—to go with the flow of this world. To live a life that is pleasing to God may mean we let go of some friendships we thought would last or let go of a romantic relationship that isn't drawing you closer to God. It might mean being outcasted by our family because they don't agree or understand our choice to have a relationship with God.

Nowhere in the Bible does it say that this walk with Him will be easy. That's one of the lies the enemy likes to use on us: "*If* you were *really* saved it shouldn't be this hard." "*If* God loves you, why are you struggling so much?" That was a big one for me. For a long time, I thought I had missed some "Christian 101" download when I first started my walk with God. I thought everyone else around me had it all together, that they didn't struggle with the same things I did. It didn't help that at that time the church I was going to didn't talk about their struggles with sin in their lives. It seemed a very hush-hush kind of topic, which only increased the isolation I felt. I was already confused at the time about God and their secrecy didn't help. I even got to the point that I struggled with thoughts of suicide because I thought I was nothing but a screwup when it came to my relationship with God.

One of the most important things I learned during that hardship in my life was that Christianity is a journey where heaven is our destination. We take different roads, but the destination is the same. God has unique plans for each of us. Some are called to be missionaries while others teachers, moms, or dads. There are soldiers, and there are those that use their hands to grow, build, or create.

This is what I mean by taking different roads. Once we accept Jesus as our savior, we're all on the "born again" road together, but some spend that walk going through the trenches in war defending their country. Others walk the road with snot, drool, food, and paint on their clothes. The road you're on may not be as bumpy as someone else's or your road may be more bumpy, but that doesn't mean either of you are doing something wrong. It's just a bump in the road.

> Yes the body has many different parts, not just one part. If the foot says, "I'm not a part of the body because I am not a hand." That does not make it any less a part of the body. And if the ear says, "I am not a part of the body because I am not an eye," would that make it any less a part of the body? If the whole body were an eye, how would you hear? Or if your whole body were an ear how would you smell anything? But our bodies have many parts, and God has put each part just where he wants it. How strange a body would be if it only had one part! Yes, there are many parts, but only one body. The eye can never say to the hand, "I don't need you." The head can't say to the feet, "I don't need you." (1 Corinthians 12:14–21 NLT)

Each of us has a unique and special part to play in this world. There is a reason God put you where you are in time, your location, and if we turn to Him for guidance, we will fulfill that purpose. There may be times you don't know what that purpose is, and that's okay. Spend that time focusing on God, and He will show you what your path is when the time is right.

As I mentioned before, we are on a journey. That journey will give us different roles in our lifetime. For part of our journey, we are a child, taken care of by our parents, raised and educated until we move out on our own. We then transition into trying to figure out what makes us unique and special and how we can impact the world in ways no other person can. This season is also where the devil likes to sneak in and attack your purpose, trying to get you to follow the world's customs and ways to prevent you from finding out what part of the body you are in God's kingdom.

Another season may be when you get married and learn how to become a wife and possibly, in time, a mother. There are those that are called to singleness—who are content to be alone, and praise God that they're content in that! They still have to navigate the path that God has for them. It's important to remember that no matter where you are on your journey, your identity must come from God. I will go into more detail on this subject in a later chapter.

I said before that this Christian walk isn't easy, but that doesn't mean that it's not worth it. Remember, Jesus told us that we would go through trials, but He also told us that we have peace in Him. There is always hope in Jesus.

3

Comfort in Loss

I wrote in the last chapter about some of the trials we may face in life. I told you how powerful your testimony can be. Allow me to share some testimonies of people who have been hit out of the blue but overcame through their relationship with God.

At roughly thirty weeks pregnant, Dawn ended up going to the hospital with severe back pain. She was given medication to stop her early labor and was put on bedrest. It was only a few weeks later that she ended up in the hospital again. She found out later on that she had a yeast infection that had gone internal as well as having the placenta detach. This caused the child that she was carrying to be stillborn. She said it was the hardest moment of her life. "You don't realize how conditioned you are to hear a baby cry until you hear that silence." Dawn told me during an interview.

There are countless women who go through the loss of a child. Most, if not all of them, carry that pain with them even if they have children after their loss. The pain of grief is something that we learn to live with and lean on God to help us through the more difficult days. Dawn was strong; within weeks, she ended up pregnant again with her second daughter.

This child also had complications with her birth, though not to the severity of her first, named Kayla. Her second was born on September 8, and it was discovered shortly after her birth she had beta-strep pneumonia. She was immediately taken into the neonatal intensive care unit where she stayed for a week and a half until Dawn was able to finally bring her home. She found out later on that beta-strep pneumonia is 100 percent fatal if untreated.

Later on down the road, when her second daughter was in school, Dawn had to fight with the school to get her evaluated for ADHD. At the time, she needed the school to agree to a child needing to be tested for a pediatrician to do the testing. After months of fighting, they finally had exhausted all the routes except to give Dawn the referral she needed. This was vital in preparing her for another fight for a later child in the educational system as well.

Her third child also had issues with her birth. Due to her being active in the womb, her third child managed to get her umbilical cord wrapped around her neck and under her arm during the labor process. Thankfully, the doctors were able to take care of the issue before anything serious happened.

Her fourth child was a son who ended up being diagnosed later on in life as high-functioning autistic with Asperger's. He was the child that she had to be an advocate for during his school years. She had to fight to make sure that he got the support that he needed to thrive. This isn't the end of Dawn's struggles and trials involving her children.

When he was seventeen years old, Dawn's son had fallen ill; his family had assumed it was simply a cold as his only complaint was of his side hurting. They let him rest, assuming his body would fight off the illness on its own. One Sunday morning, his eldest sister felt an urge she couldn't brush away to check on him.

She had plans that afternoon and just arrived home from church. She was making some lunch when she heard a voice tell her, *"Go check on your brother."* She brushed it off with the thought *I'll go check on him in a minute. I'm hungry.* The voice spoke again, this time, louder: *"Go check on him* now,*"* leaving her no room for argument this time around.

When she made her way into his room, she noticed that he was nonresponsive. He was breathing, but his eyes were open, and his skin color was faded. She tried shaking his shoulder, calling out his name and tapping his face, hoping for some kind of reaction. Nothing.

Making her way out into the living room where her mother was, she asked if she'd checked on him earlier in the day. Dawn said she had; her daughter then informed her that her brother wasn't responding. Dawn quickly made her way into the room. At first, she thought he wasn't breathing but quickly realized he was. She told her daughter to call 911 while she raced to get her husband.

Everything raced from there: The paramedics had to carry him from the house on his bedsheet as the gurney wouldn't fit into the house. Dawn rode with them in the ambulance while her husband took the car and drove behind them. He was rushed to the hospital, and the doctors asked her if he'd done any drugs or had drank any alcohol. She told them no; he was a good kid who stayed home and played video games. At this point, she was terrified as to what was going on with her son.

Shortly after his arrival, the doctors came and told her that his blood sugar level was at 1,515. They said his blood was like syrup in his veins. He was in the pediatric ICU, but at six feet tall, they had to bring an adult bed in from the regular hospital area in order to fit him. During the first night she spent in the hospital with him, he was in a medically induced coma and was in that condition for a day and a half.

While he was in his coma, she spoke to him and told him to follow her voice and wake up. His family came to visit him the first night in the hospital, and his eldest sister prayed over him, speaking Bible scriptures—even though she wasn't well versed in how to do so during times like these. Dawn also prayed over him, that God would help him use his newly diagnosed diabetes for God's glory.

The son had diabetic ketoacidosis and also got pneumonia while in the hospital. Once he was released, thanks to his autism, he was able to work his medication schedule into his life with relative ease. He learned how to do his own injections as well as record his numbers.

He is thriving even after his life-threatening scare. It is unsure if he remembers much while he was in his coma; he doesn't like to talk about it, but I believe that he heard our mom and myself praying over him.

Dawn is my mother. She has been through a lot in her life, but she's held strong through it all. She's been through divorce, the loss of a child, the near loss of three others, and the loss of a great-niece, as well as the trials that come through everyday life.

There are situations in life that can leave you asking "why." and sometimes the answer to that is "I don't know." We live in a fallen world, and sometimes there are casualties because of that. Things happen that we simply can't explain this side of heaven, but we have to believe that God is working those things for His glory.

One scripture in the Bible is two words long. and that is John 11:35 (Amplified Bible), which says, "Jesus wept." Jesus was a man that brought people back from the dead, healed blind eyes, healed those whom society had cast out. He was 100 percent God and 100 percent human. He felt the same emotions we feel; he didn't deny them or call any particular emotion "evil" nor were any of the emotions he experienced sinful as Jesus never sinned.

> This High Priest of ours understands our weakness, for he faced all the same testings we do, yet he did not sin. (Hebrews 4:15 NLT)

> And you know that Jesus came to take away our sins, and there is no sin in him. (1 John 3:5 NLT)

> For God made Christ, who never sinned, to be the offering for our sin, so that we could be made right with God through Christ. (2 Corinthians 5:21 NLT)

There are times that we may feel that Jesus isn't able to understand what we go through because our times are so different from the culture he experienced while walking the earth. If we really get to the root of it, though, it isn't that different. Children died too young back then, and they still do today. There are still evils in this world just as there were in His time, and there will continue to be after our time until Jesus returns.

Loss is a difficult subject to talk about for many people. It's something almost everyone has dealt with in one form or another. Whether it's the loss of a friendship, a relationship, the loss of a parent, sibling, or child. It all tears at our heart and can make us feel like we're drowning in the darkest ocean waves.

> He always comes alongside us to comfort us
> in every suffering so that we can come alongside
> those who are in any painful trial. We can bring
> them this same comfort that God has poured out
> upon us. (2 Corinthians 1:4 TPT)

In times of loss, it can become so easy to isolate ourselves, but isolation is one of the worst things we can do to ourselves. It can be so easy to want to curl up on our own, to nurse the pain deep inside our hearts. We don't want to let anyone else in for fear that the pain will grow worse, or someone will validate the lies we hear during that time from the enemy: "I could have done something," "It's my fault," "I'll never get over this," "This pain will never go away." If the enemy can isolate us in this vulnerable time, he will have an easier time keeping us in the dark, therefore keeping power over us.

There will be times when it seems like the darkness is all that we can see. We can feel lost in pain, and the transition from the life we lived before the loss to the new life we now live in. It's difficult, but it's not impossible. No one plans to suffer through a divorce, a miscarriage, loss of a family member, or other circumstances that may blindside us. We plan for the happier things in our life: our children, or nieces, nephews growing up and fulfilling the dreams they have, growing old with the person we made a lifelong commitment to, being able to fulfill our own dreams in life.

We are not alone in these difficult seasons even if we may feel like we are. Others can share their experiences with us, but sadly, few are willing to be vulnerable enough and transparent enough to let others see that their life isn't all sunshine and rainbows. That there were and are times they doubted, and at times, they struggled to understand why. The particular question "why" may never be answered this side of heaven.

These types of situations doesn't make God any less good. One thing to remember is that God's thoughts are higher than our thoughts. We may not know how, but God will use all things for our good. He will find a way to use the weapons of pain and loss the devil tries to use to break us and use them to propel us forward. The devil wants us bound while God wants us free. God can use the enemy's weapon against him and use our testimony that once was meant to destroy us to inspire others and set them free as well.

> So we are convinced that every detail of our
> lives is continually woven together for good, for
> we are his lovers who have been called to fulfill
> his designed purpose. (Romans 8:25 TPT)

One of the hardest parts with writing this book was opening up about my struggles, my past, my pain. Part of that has to do with the society we live in. They say there's always someone else that is struggling more than you are. This is true, but that doesn't make your pain any less real or any less heavy to bear.

I also struggled with the idea of how others would respond to hearing about parts of my life that I didn't openly, freely talk about. There were only a few people in my life that knew the depth of how deep my struggles reached.

Fear of how others respond to our testimony can be extremely binding. Remember that this is exactly why the devil uses this tactic, to immobilize us. By doing so, we are allowing them to place value on our actions—for better or for worse. We can't go back and change those things about our story; however, those things do not have to define us.

I have someone I love dearly in my life, and she made a wrong choice some time ago. There were times afterward that it seemed like she was holding onto that choice as if it would define her for the rest of her life. It broke my heart to see her doing that, but it began to make me wonder how often we do that with our own. Even when I spoke with her, it took many months of prayers for God to open her eyes to the reality of the situation, that she couldn't change it, but it didn't define how He felt about her either.

How often do we falsely believe the circumstances of our past dictate who we will become in the future? Who we hope to be, what we hope to do. How often do we look to that in our lives to determine our value? We believe that our mistakes, circumstances, or events define us more than what God says about us; and that is a dangerous road to be on.

Ouch. I'm speaking to myself as much as I am speaking to you about this. These things only have power in our lives if we allow them to. You can learn from them and move on, but too often, we refuse to learn from them, or we simply hold onto them as if they're too valuable to let go.

God doesn't make mistakes. He made you just the way He wanted you to be. Your personality, your quirks, what makes you distinctly different, it's all chosen by God; and He loves you. Your mistakes or choices you regret doesn't change that.

There are a few things Jesus offers us in these times. One of the most important things is hope. Today may have been the hardest day you may have ever gone through, but there is always hope for a better tomorrow in Jesus.

> And this hope will not lead to disappointment. For we know how dearly God loves us, because he has given us the Holy Spirit to fill our hearts with his love. (Romans 5:5 NLT)

> I pray that God, the source of hope, will fill you completely with joy and peace because you trust in Him. Then you will overflow with confident hope through the power of the Holy Spirit. (Romans 15:13 NLT)

> But those who trust in the Lord will find
> new strength. They will soar high on wings like
> eagles. They will run and not grow weary. They
> will walk and not faint. (Isaiah 40:31 NLT)

There are times it is hard to hope, especially when it seems like everything around us is crumbling. We are offered hope, peace, and even joy during difficult seasons in our lives through Jesus. There will be times when it feels that we have lost our hope, our joy, or our peace; but if we press into God, we will receive all that and more. It is a choice we must make for ourselves.

There is a woman in my church who I once believed had an amazing relationship with God. I assumed—keyword there—that she grew up as a good Christian girl and was raised to walk with God from a young age. I found out that all too often we look at people especially those older than us, and assume that if they've got a strong relationship with God, they had a good, strong foundation since they were young. This woman, and another woman I interviewed and will speak about later, did not.

As this woman shared her story with me over milkshakes, I was really taken aback at what she'd gone through and just how far God had brought her. I will say that this was when I learned that assuming something about someone else's story will not help your faith. She was kind enough to be transparent and share some of her history with me.

Jenn and I shared a similar history. She was also molested by a babysitter at the age of five; her mother noticed it quickly enough to end it before it went on too long, but she told me about how she repressed her feelings about it until she was in her twenties.

Jenn told me about how her mother was an alcoholic and into drugs, that she herself fell into the same kind of habit and took pills as well. This continued until she was pregnant, and she realized she had to change in order to protect the baby.

At the time, she and her husband had been into drugs; they had managed to get themselves into trouble with the Asian mafia and had to go on the run from them with their child. It was during this time that Jenn told me that things began to change. She began to focus on her relationships putting God first then her husband and her children after that. Once they were safe and able to have a stable home life, Jenn and her husband agreed to go to marriage counseling as well as dedicating one year to church.

Jenn told me about how she had struggled with finding a church that she felt would accept her and her family. She ended up at the same church I now attend and fell in love with the pastor for the same reason I did: He was transparent about his history and offered hope to those that needed it. She and her family have been attending the church for fifteen years, and her eldest child even attended Bible college through the church. She credits my pastor's honesty and openness with how much stronger her relationship with God has gotten alongside her own work on her relationship with God as well.

Over the years, I've come to realize there are many people who suffer losses that most of us—thankfully—couldn't comprehend. From the mother who lost a child before she even took her first breath to the woman who cares for her husband's every need due to a tragic accident while raising their children, to the woman who had to go into hiding to protect her family. There are so many more stories of people who have faced the darkest of times and have overcome, not through their own power but by the power of Christ in them!

Thus far, I have shared some of my own stories: my issues with molestation and suicidal thoughts that I fought for many years. There was a recent, painful event in my life shortly before I began writing this book that occurred—one that shook me to my core. It shook my faith down to its foundation

Let me take you back to February 2012. One of my stepsisters was due to have her first child, a girl. Little did I know at the time just how much that fiery bundle of joy would change my life.

I saw my newest niece quite often as my sister lived just down the street from where I was attending college at the time. My sister had medical issues that made it difficult for her when my niece was young. I would take the sweet little one to give my sister a break, and I loved every minute of being an aunt to her.

As the years passed, the bond between the two of us deepened. There was nothing that made my heart happier than hearing her call me "Auntie Tasha!" She held my heart, and I never wanted it back. She made me proud to be an aunt, and she inspired me to become better each day. The simple love of a child inspired me to grow so I could be a good example for her to look up to when she was older.

My mom and I would take her on trips to the beach, and we would take her to go horseback riding, which she fell in love with quickly. I remember the first time she got to ride on a horse herself. She remembered the horse's name: Bella. She felt so grown-up when she was able to ride on her own every time we made a trip to the beach.

We took her to concerts; she even got a T-shirt signed by a band she was in love with, and the leader of the band hugged her and kissed the top of her head. The band was Newsboys. She was on cloud nine after that particular concert! Most importantly, we took her to church.

It felt like I blinked, and she went from being in the nursery chatting with the then-worship leader's son to the four-year-old room and then to the elementary school classes downstairs. Two girls, sisters, quickly became best friends with her. They were like sisters with my niece, and the three of them were always so excited to see each other on the Sundays I brought her to church. My niece also connected with the girls' younger brother and doted on him whenever she saw him. She was like an honorary member of that family.

The bond grew deeper every time they got to spend time together. She had such a bright light, such a heart for God and for people. Eventually, I decided to go to Bible school because of my desire to grow and shine as she did. I began to understand the scripture about coming to God with the heart of a child.

> And said, "I assure you and most solemnly
> say to you, unless you repent [that is, change
> your inner self—your old way of thinking, live
> changed lives] and become like children [trust-

ing, humble, and forgiving], you will never enter
the kingdom of heaven." (Matthew 18:3 AMP)

So many plans were made, so many hopes and dreams for what she would do with her life. The saying that tomorrow isn't promised has never been more true than on that night I got an unexpected phone call.

One tragic night, all that hope, all those plans, those dreams, all of it was ripped away. While out on the sidewalk with her mom and two-year-old sister, a car jumped the curb and hit all three of them. I got the news about the accident and started praying. At the time, I didn't know that they had been walking on the sidewalk. I thought they were in a car with a friend and assumed they would all be okay.

I was on the phone with one of the ladies from my church explaining what was going on and asking for prayer when I got the news. My eldest niece was gone. That bright, vibrant, sassy, loving light was gone.

I couldn't comprehend it. She couldn't be gone. The doctors had to have mixed her up with someone else. She wasn't supposed to go like this. She was supposed to grow up; she was supposed to live her life. I refused to believe the news. I asked my stepmom who had told her that they had to be lying. It was then she told me that a police officer had been the one to inform her and my niece's mom. She was gone.

I felt numb, and it took a few moments for my mind to fully catch up with the news. I couldn't believe it. It was just moments after that I found out she didn't make it off of the scene of the accident. It was then that I learned that they hadn't been in a car as I had thought; they had been hit while walking to a bus stop.

At that moment, I had never felt such pain rip through me. It felt as if all of my insides were being ripped out through my chest. I fell to my knees, and in that moment, I begged God to be with me, to hold me through this pain. I knew I couldn't survive this without Him.

While processing everything that had happened, I had to inform other family members and members of my church about the news I'd received. First, I told my uncle who lived next door to me at the time.

All I wanted to do was fall apart with him, but I couldn't yet. I called my mom and told her next. I can still hear her screaming. I couldn't scream no matter how badly I wanted to.

I knew I couldn't go through this pain alone, so I called a coworker and friend; though she lived a good distance away, she still raced over to my house as well as a friend from church who also rushed into town. I contacted my grandparents and could barely get the news out to them; I was feeling so broken I couldn't stand and had to sit on the step outside my front door as I tried to gather my words together that their great-granddaughter was gone.

Telling the teachers from church—who all adored my niece—was especially difficult. One of those teachers was the mother to the two girls she'd become especially close to. She had to inform her daughters of the loss. With each person I had to tell about the loss, it felt like the pain was growing stronger; it was becoming more real with each person I talked to.

My roommate was the last person I had the energy to contact. She screamed for me over the phone. She screamed in the way I so badly wanted to but couldn't.

The loss was a devastating loss to so many people who loved her. Not only to her family, but to those that had watched her grow over the years, the lives that she touched in many ways. The loss had a ripple effect.

My pastor's wife reached out shortly after hearing the news, and that alone meant the world to me; to have people reaching out in the darkest moment of my life helped me breathe a little more each time, so I didn't feel like I was going to suffocate while trying to hold myself together. I had people I could lean on; I didn't have to go through this loss alone.

I can honestly say I don't know where I would be today if it wasn't for my faith and my church. The day after the accident was a Sunday. I went to church; even through all that pain, I knew I needed to be there. It was there that I got filled and got the support to make it through the struggles life had thrown at me before. I needed that more now than ever.

The hugs I got that day were what helped piece me back together. With physical touch being my love language, it felt as if each hug took a little bit of the weight off of my shoulders. The first hug was from a mentor and friend. She's a mom of many kids—all who are grown—and the moment I hugged her, I could feel the weight coming off of me. I could breathe a little easier. She had the mom type of hug that I so desperately needed. The next person to hug me was one of my niece's favorite teachers. Her hug too was exactly what I had needed in that moment. With each hug, I felt like I wasn't going to be crushed under that burden of pain. As long as I reached out to those that wanted to support me.

As difficult as the loss of my niece was, it rekindled a friendship that had waned a few years before as well. That friend, I had decided to walk away from the friendship a few years prior due to the fact that as much as I loved her, she was going down a path that was not one that was going to pull her closer to God.

She had changed since our time apart and had returned to God by the time we reconnected. It broke her heart as much as it had anyone else that knew my niece, but we were able to find comfort and connection again through the loss.

This particular friend had a son that also adored my niece. When the two of them were younger, they had hit it off quite quickly in their friendship, and he was devastated when he found out about her passing. As I saw just how many lives my niece had affected in her short life, it inspired me to do more, to be stronger. She was so young, only nine, but she had impacted so many people in her short time on earth.

There are still days that it hurts. I won't lie to you about that. There are days I have to call out to God, asking Him to be there, to hold me up in His hands, and He does. The steps are painful, and as holidays pass, it gets stirred up now and again. It won't overwhelm me, however. This is because I have put my foundation in Jesus, not the things of this world. Even through the greatest of pain, God understands. Leaning on Him is the best way to make it through those painful times that come our way.

So now you Gentiles are no longer strangers and foreigners. You are citizens along with all of God's holy people. You are members of God's family. Together, we are his house, built on the foundation of the apostles and the prophets. And the cornerstone is Christ Jesus himself. (Ephesians 2:19–20 NLT)

There were a few scriptures I spoke over myself during this time—ones of comfort, of hope. Psalm 23 (NLT) was one I focused on a lot.

The Lord is my shepherd;
I have all that I need.
He lets me rest in green meadows;
he leads me beside peaceful streams.
He renews my strength.
He guides me along right paths,
bringing honor to his name.
Even when I walk
through the darkest valley,
I will not be afraid,
for you are close beside me.
Your rod and your staff
protect and comfort me.
You prepare a feast for me
in the presence of my enemies.
You honor me by anointing my head with oil.
My cup overflows with blessings.
Surely your goodness and unfailing love will pursue me
all the days of my life,
and I will live in the house of the Lord
Forever.

There were times I didn't want to pray; I couldn't listen to worship music without breaking down again. Some of the songs I remember watching her dance around to or singing in the car. I couldn't listen to Newsboys or Francesca Battistelli for a few weeks after the loss. With God's help, I was able to listen to some of the songs she rocked out to again, but it took time.

When those moments of pain came, I had to accept the emotion I was feeling, recognize that it was painful, but press on into God and trust that He would bring me through it. I didn't know how God was going to use this tragedy for His glory, but I had to believe that He would. What the enemy planned for harm, God would turn around for His good.

> You intended to harm me, but God intended it all for good. He brought me to this position so I could save the lives of many people. (Genesis 50:20 NLT)

My niece had a heart for people during her time on earth. She would give away clothes that didn't fit her to her friends and always seemed to be looking for a way to lift someone else's life, to show God's love to them through her actions.

For her celebration of life, my mom and I decided to ask people to bring dresses for girls in the foster care system instead of flowers. We wanted to do something special in her memory, something that she would've wanted to have done. One of the ladies at the church had a friend who worked in the foster care field and could deliver the dresses for us. Before and after the celebration, we prayed that each girl who got a dress would feel like a princess and that God would show them love through these gifts.

This sweet young girl touched so many lives in her nine short years. She inspired those around her not by her amazing accomplishments, not by her astounding knowledge or stunning beauty, but by the love that she showed the least fortunate. She loved passing out things to the homeless in town. For a while, she and I would make scarves then we moved to cereal bars. She gave with a smile on her face and showed God's love.

> Let your light shine before men in such
> a way that they may see your good deeds and
> moral excellence, and [recognize and honor and]
> glorify your Father who is in heaven. (Matthew
> 5:16 AMP)

There may be times we may not understand why something is happening in our lives. I have seen young women lose their husbands unexpectedly, mothers and fathers lose their children, children lose their parents. In the middle of the storm, it's so easy to try and isolate yourself, to try and curl up to keep the pain at bay. It won't help you. I speak from experience. The pain can make you feel like you'll never make it to the other side, that this is where your life falls apart, but God has greater plans for you.

Choosing to worship Him in the storm isn't an easy choice, but it's one of the best ones you can make as you will be setting your foundation on the rock that is Jesus instead of the sand, which is anything else this world may offer to dull the pain.

If you're suffering through a loss, I encourage you to reach out to those close to you. Reach out to friends, family, church members, someone. Don't allow yourself to fall into the trap of isolation while you're in pain.

The pain of loss doesn't disqualify you from being used by God either. As much as the enemy may tell you otherwise, God can still use you.

The Bible shares those who have hurt through loss, but one powerful and heartbreaking story is the story of Mary, the mother of Jesus.

> In the sixth month of Elizabeth's pregnancy,
> God sent the angel Gabriel to Nazareth, a vil-
> lage in Galilee, to a virgin named Mary. She was
> engaged to be married to a man named Joseph,

a descendant of King David. Gabriel appeared to her and said, "Greetings, favored woman! The Lord is with you!" Confused and disturbed, Mary tried to think what the angel could mean. "Don't be afraid, Mary," the angel told her, "for you have found favor with God! You will conceive and give birth to a son, and you will name him Jesus. He will be very great and will be called the Son of the Most High. The Lord God will give him the throne of his ancestor David. And he will reign over Israel forever; his Kingdom will never end!" Mary asked the angel, "But how can this happen? I am a virgin." The angel replied, "The Holy Spirit will come upon you, and the power of the Most High will overshadow you. So the baby to be born will be holy, and he will be called the Son of God. What's more, your relative Elizabeth has become pregnant in her old age! People used to say she was barren, but she has conceived a son and is now in her sixth month. For the word of God will never fail." Mary responded, "I am the Lord's servant. May everything you have said about me come true." And then the angel left her. (Luke 1:26–38 NLT)

Mary was thrown for a loop from the very beginning. She wasn't even married yet, and an angel came to her and told her that she would carry a child while still a virgin. Most of us probably would have been more skeptical, but Mary chose to have faith believing in what God said he would do through the angel.

So Joseph also went up from the town of Nazareth in Galilee to Judea, to Bethlehem the town of David, because he belonged to the house and line of David. He went there to register with Mary, who was pledged to be married to him and was expecting a child. While they were there, the time came for the baby to be born, and she gave birth to her firstborn, a son. She wrapped him in cloths and placed him in a manger, because there was no guest room available for them. And there were shepherds living out in the fields nearby, keeping watch over their flocks at night. An angel of the Lord appeared to them, and the glory of the Lord shone around them, and they were terrified. But the angel said to them, "Do not be afraid. I bring you good news that will cause great joy for all the people. Today in the town of David a Savior has been born to you; he is the Messiah, the Lord. This will be a sign to you: You will find a baby wrapped in cloths and lying in a manger." Suddenly a great company of the heavenly host appeared with the angel, praising God and saying, "Glory to God in the highest heaven, and on earth peace to those on whom his favor rests." When the angels had left them and gone into heaven, the shepherds said to one another, "Let's go to Bethlehem and see this thing that has happened, which the Lord has told us about." So they hurried off and found Mary and Joseph, and the baby, who was lying in the manger. When they had seen him, they spread the word concerning what had been told them about this child, and all who heard it were amazed at what the shepherds said to them. But Mary treasured up all these things and pondered them in her heart. The shepherds returned, glorifying and praising God for all the things they had heard and seen, which were just as they had been told. (Luke 2:4–20 NIV)

Jesus was born to her just as the angels had said. While she had been informed about her child, she had no idea what he would do with his life. She couldn't have guessed the miracles he would work, the people he would heal, the lives he would change, or the death that he would endure at a relatively young age. There's no scripture that shares the age Jesus was when he died, but he was believed to be in his midthirties.

> Pilate let Barabbas go free but he had men whip Jesus. Then he handed Him over to be nailed to a cross. (Matthew 27:26 NLT)

The whipping that Jesus endured wasn't just with a whip. He was almost unrecognizable as a person. The whips they used had bits of rock, metal, anything that would cause more harm to the person being whipped. Jesus endured all this torture before he was even nailed to the cross.

Imagine the pain Mary had to endure watching her eldest son being tortured and killed while he was innocent of any wrongdoing. Remember, earlier, the angel had called Mary favored. This favor, however, did not save her from the suffering she had to endure as well.

Mary was warned of this when Jesus was young. When they brought Jesus to the temple, a man named Simeon spoke with Mary and Joseph.

> Then Simeon blessed them, and he said to Mary, the baby's mother, "This child is destined to cause many in Israel to fall, and many others to rise. He has been sent as a sign from God, but many will oppose him. As a result, the deepest thoughts of many hearts will be revealed. And a sword will pierce your very soul." (Luke 2:34–35 NLT)

God was able to use Mary's loss for a greater good. It's incredibly difficult to see how God may use something as horrible as what

Mary went through to bring glory to His name, but God has a way of turning things around. The most important part to remember is to hold onto God through that time as Mary did. Even though she lost her child, Mary didn't blame God. She relied on Him to help her through the pain she was experiencing. We can do the same.

4

The Comparison Trap

I spoke in the previous chapter about how I had assumed things about people's lives based on where they were when I met them. It was when I started having a relationship with some of the women in my church that I realized that I had been comparing my lowlights, my mistakes and shortcomings, to their highlights. I had no idea what their journey had cost them, what they had gone through in order to be where they were at that time in their lives, yet I compared my valley to their mountaintop.

Comparison is another one of the biggest traps we can fall into quite easily. We can compare ourselves to just about anyone; it doesn't even have to be someone we know personally. How often have we compared our life to the life of a celebrity?

This is one of the tricks the enemy tries to use on us to cause us to become stagnant, to keep us from moving forward toward the goal that God has for our lives. We compare ourselves with those we see in magazines, those we see in positions of authority in church, people we pass on the street, see at school, even our own family members.

We compare ourselves to other people's actions we see as accomplishments: marriage, being single, owning a home, having an "ideal" job, having children or being childless, having an education or certain degree, having a close-knit family—the list goes on.

We often compare ourselves to their appearances, their personalities or how they present themselves to others. How often do we truly know beyond the layer that we see? Many times, we don't see the road that lead that person to where they are in that moment that we're comparing ourselves to them.

One important thing to remember when fighting against the urge to compare ourselves to others is the fact that God created each and every one of us as unique. Not even twins are identical in every way. They may live in the same household, but they don't share the same experiences. They may share the same DNA, but their fingerprints are unique to each of them.

Another thing to remember, as I mentioned before, is that we're only getting a glimpse of that person's life—a highlight. We don't see what goes on behind closed doors, nor do we know what that person's history is like.

When we compare ourselves to others, we are taking all our story—the stuff we like and dislike about ourselves and how we came to be—and comparing them with the highlights of someone else's life. We put the other person on a pedestal without knowing the grime and gunk they have gone through in their own lives to get to where they are.

I will say that I have been guilty of doing this in the past, and there are times I still do. Overcoming this is a journey that we're on, and that journey is one step at a time.

One choice we can make that will help in this journey to freedom from comparison is to read the Bible and look up scriptures that explain what God thinks of you. Dig in deep and see how much love, how much time, effort, dedication He put into creating you.

You have a story that only you can tell; you can reach people in your circle that others wouldn't have the same impact with. Your life, regardless of how it began, the bumps in the road that happened along the way, or how far off you may be from where you think you should be, is important. Your life is important to God. He has a plan and a purpose for your life. Do not allow the enemy to steal that fact from you.

Our emotions can make us feel one way when the facts say another. This is when you need to dig deep into the Word of God and allow His Truth to surround you.

> "For I know the plans I have for you," says the Lord. "They are plans for good and not for disaster, to give you a future and a hope. In those days when you pray, I will listen. If you look for me wholeheartedly, you will find me. I will be found by you." Says the Lord. "I will end your captivity and restore your fortunes. I will gather you out of the nations where I sent you and bring you home again to your own land." (Jeremiah 29:11–14 NLT)

God has a plan for you. His plan isn't for your life to be a disaster. We live in a world that suffers, and we must suffer at times as a result of the fall. That doesn't mean that God's plans for your life aren't good. Jesus didn't promise that life would be all sunshine and rainbows after being a Christian.

There were those who stood strong in their faith after Jesus ascended to heaven and suffered horrible deaths, but they refused to give up on their faith because they knew that God was the only way to heaven. There are so many stories in the Bible where God used people that no one else would've ever thought were "worthy" or "qualified" for their position.

Let's look into the story of one man that went from persecuting Christians to being one. His story is one of the most inspirational transformation stories out there! We'll start with a man named Stephen, as this was the beginning of Paul's story:

> "You stubborn people! You are heathens at heart and deaf to the truth. Must you forever resist the Holy Spirit? That's what your ancestors did, and so do you! Name one prophet your ancestors didn't persecute! They even killed the ones who predicted the coming of the Righteous One—the Messiah whom you betrayed and murdered. You deliberately disobeyed God's law even though you received it from the hands of angels."

The Jewish leaders were infuriated by Stephen's accusations and they shook their fists at him in rage. But Stephen, full of the Holy Spirit, gazed steadily into heaven and saw the glory of God, and he saw Jesus standing in the place of honor at God's right hand. And he told them, "Look, I see the heavens opened and the Son of Man standing in the place of honor at God's right hand!" Then they put their hands over their ears and began shouting. They rushed at him and dragged him out of the city and began to stone him. His accusers took off their coats and laid them at the feet of a young man named Saul. As they stoned him, Stephen prayed, "Lord Jesus, receive my spirit." He fell to his knees shouting, "Lord, don't charge them with this sin!" And with that, he died. Saul was one of the witnesses, and he agreed completely with the killing of Stephen. A great wave of persecution began that day, sweeping over the church in Jerusalem; and all the believers except the apostles were scattered through the regions of Judea and Samaria. (Some devout men came and buried Stephen with great mourning.) But Saul was going everywhere to destroy the church. He went from house to house, dragging out both men and women to throw them into prison. (Acts 7:51–8:3 NLT)

This was the beginning of the story of the man who would go on to write 28 percent of the New Testament. You can see in the scriptures above there was no compassion, no grace in the way Paul handled things. It didn't matter if you were a man or a woman; he would throw you into prison simply for being a Christian and believing that Jesus was the Son of God. He didn't care about their belief; he had been trained in the way of religious law since he was young. To him, he was doing God's work.

Meanwhile, Saul was uttering threats with every breath and was eager to kill the Lord's followers. So he went to the high priest. He requested letters addressed to the synagogues in Damascus, asking for their cooperation in the arrest of any followers of the Way he found there. He wanted to bring them—both men and women—back to Jerusalem in chains. As he was approaching Damascus on this mission, a light from heaven suddenly shone down around him. He fell to the ground and heard a voice saying to him, "Saul! Saul! Why are you persecuting me?" "Who are you, lord?" Saul asked. And the voice replied, "I am Jesus, the one you are persecuting! Now get up and go into the city, and you will be told what you must do." The men with Saul stood speechless, for they heard the sound of someone's voice but saw no one! Saul picked himself up off the ground, but when he opened his eyes he was blind. So his companions lead him by the hand to Damascus. He remained there blind for three days and did not eat or drink. (Acts 9:1–9 NLT)

My mind wonders what Saul had to be thinking about during those three days of being blind. I'm sure he believed in Jesus quickly after what had happened to him, but he'd been on a mission to imprison Christians. He even supported the death of them simply for believing in Jesus. Most would assume that God couldn't use someone that was so far on the warpath. One would assume that God would choose someone who was closer to His heart, someone that loved His people as God loved them. God's plans don't always go as we think they should. He has a habit of using those we least expect in the most impactful ways.

But the Lord said, "Go, for Saul is my chosen instrument to take my message to the Gentiles and kings, as well as to the people of Israel. And I will show him how much he must suffer for my namesake." So Ananias went and found Saul. He laid his hands on him and said, 'Brother Saul, the Lord Jesus, who appeared to you on the road, has sent me so that you might regain your sight and be filled with the Holy Spirit." Instantly something like scales fell from Saul's eyes, and he regained his sight. Then he got up and was baptized. Afterward he ate some food and regained his strength. Saul stayed with the believers in Damascus for a few days. And immediately he began preaching about Jesus in the synagogues saying, "He is indeed the Son of God!" All who heard him were amazed. "Isn't this the same man who caused such devastation among Jesus' followers in Jerusalem?" they asked. "And didn't he come here to arrest them and take them in chains to the leading priests?" (Acts 9:15–21 NLT)

"Wasn't she a drug addict?" "Wasn't he a thief?" "Didn't she lose her virginity at prom?" Whatever your past was, it no longer gets to define you. A man who encouraged the murder of Christians and caused devastation in their faith was used by God in a way that left people scratching their heads. God will use you the same way as well.

Our calling from God is uniquely ours. No one gets the same calling we do; no one gets to say we're underqualified because we don't have an education or we're disqualified because of the choices in our past. God is the one that calls us by name. God is the one who knows the plans He has for our lives. If He is for you, who can be against you? Even the Jews in Damascus tried to plot to kill Paul after he changed his ways.

There will be those that will try to sabotage your change as well; you don't have to let them. You can let go of what used to define you. You can stop comparing your mess to someone else's success. Life is not a competition. No one wins overall because they got more degrees, didn't fight with their husband or children as much as others, or anything we tend to use to rise ourselves above others. The prize at the end of this life is Jesus, but only if we accept Him and His sacrifice for us.

Comparisons will steal your joy. It will steal your hope, and it will steal the assurance you have for your salvation. There were many times in my early years as a Christian that I thought that I had to be sinless, perfect to have a relationship with God. I thought that because of my history, I was disqualified from being used by God. I would look at others and compare my merk and gunk to their shining light without understanding what they had gone through to get to that point in their lives. I didn't believe I had the light of God in me because I was still struggling with sin in my life.

It wasn't until I heard the stories of those I once compared myself to that I began to realize that I wasn't alone. I wasn't the only one who had addiction in their life. I wasn't the only one that was confused and felt like they'd missed the Christian handbook when they got saved.

Comparison can steal your future as well if you let it. Too often, when we allow comparisons to weigh us down, we begin to feel that there's no way out, no hope. This can lead to depression, and sadly, some people end up taking their own lives because they've allowed their failure—or foreseen failure—to decide their worth.

Start fighting back today. Decide that today is the day you're putting your foot down and turning a different corner. There will be days you fall back into it, and when they do, pick yourself up, dust yourself off, and move on with your life. Recognize that you're not perfect, but you serve a God who is and who is with you through it all. Keep moving forward even when you trip up, and you'll get closer to your destination each time. You win if you don't give up.

As I stated before, when we compare ourselves with others, we often miss one important fact: Our value does not come by our accomplishments in life. Our value doesn't come from being a mother, having a high-ranking job, having a three-story home, being debt-free, or any other "successes" in life we may run after.

We don't have to earn our salvation, and we don't have to earn our value. We are valuable because God sees us as valuable, and He *says* we are valuable! What peace and joy that fact brings when it finally sinks in!

> Don't you realize that your body is the temple of the Holy Spirit, who lives in you and was given to you by God? You do not belong to yourself, for God bought you with a high price. So you must honor God with your body. (1 Corinthians 6:19–20 NLT)

Notice what this verse doesn't say: God paid a high price so you'd better shape up and act like it. Nor does it say God paid a high price so see yourself as filthy, count your mistakes, define your own value yourself based on your circumstances and history. No. It says your body is the temple of the Holy Spirit.

The Holy Spirit is the helper that God gives us to guide us through this life. The Holy Spirit is exactly that, holy. If it resides in you, then that means that you are holy as well, not for what you do or do not do but simply because God calls you holy. You were bought with a high price: Jesus's life. Jesus laid his life down for you. He chose to because he loves you and values you for who you are.

> What is the price of five sparrows—two copper coins? Yet God does not forget a single one of them. And the very hairs on your head are numbered. So don't be afraid; you are more valuable to God than a whole flock of sparrows. (Luke 12:6–7 NLT)

> And if God cares so wonderfully for wildflowers that are here today and thrown into the fire tomorrow, he will certainly care for you. Why do you have so little faith? (Matthew 6:30 NLT)

Some may say, "I don't have little faith. It's just how I am." or "It's being realistic." No. You can call it what you want, but when you doubt your worth, it's exactly that: doubt. That is the opposite of faith. If God says something about you, who are you to turn around and argue with Him? I'm speaking just as much to myself as I am to you.

Often, we find it easy to fall into the trap of comparison. Sometimes we do it without even realizing that we're doing it! That's why the devil loves to use it against us. Remember, his purpose is to steal, kill, and destroy. If he can destroy your view on yourself, you won't believe anything God says about you, and it won't be long before you believe that you have to prove something in order to be saved. This can cause a ripple effect as you'll then affect others around you making them believe that they need to prove themselves to God, which will pull them away from God instead of to God, which is what the enemy wants.

It's important to take the time to recognize the enemy's tactics against us so we're prepared to fight back. Our greatest weapon is the Word of God. It is what gives us strength when we are weakest, but we must fill ourselves with the Word of God before we go into battle; it will do us little good being in the midst of battle and realizing we need the Word of God to help us fight. That would be like going into battle without a sword and then having to take the time to find a weapon that will last the battle.

If you're in a battle right now, don't be dismayed. There are so many amazing ways to get scriptures to help you to fight back it's never too late. One thing rings true through the entire Bible, and that is the fact that God will never leave you nor forsake you. He is there with you in the midst of the battle. He is fighting alongside you!

So we can say with confidence, "The Lord is my helper, so I will have no fear. What can mere people do to me?" (Hebrews 13:6 NLT)

Don't be afraid, for I am with you. Don't be discouraged, for I am your God. I will strengthen you and help you. I will hold you up with my victorious right hand. (Isaiah 41:10 NLT)

Let all who fear the Lord repeat: "His faithful love endures forever." In my distress I prayed to the Lord, and the Lord answered me and set me free. The Lord is for me, so I will have no fear. What can mere people do to me? Yes, the Lord is for me, he will help me. I will look in triumph at those who hate me. It is better to take refuge in the Lord than to trust in people. It is better to take refuge in the Lord than trust in princes." (Psalm 118:4–9 NLT)

Do not gloat over me, my enemies! For though I fall, I will rise again. Though I sit in darkness, the LORD will be my light. (Micah 7:8 NLT)

God is on our side. He will never leave us. No matter how difficult or how lengthy the battle may be. Allow yourself to let that information sink in. Let it sink in past all the lies you've heard over your lifetime.

God is with you.

He loves you.

He wants you.

He desires you.

He created you.

You are precious to Him.

Nothing you do will ever change the way He feels about you.

Beloved, allow His words to sink in deep into your heart and dispel the lies hidden there. It may take some time for the roots of those lies to be pulled out of your spirit, but it will be amazing when they are.

I remember being at a ladies' night at my church a few years ago. I had been dealing with some deeply rooted issues and had been asking for God to help uproot them. During the night, we had a guest speaker, and it felt like everything she was saying was being said right to me. When she began to pray for the arrows of the enemy to be pulled out of our spirit, I could *physically* feel these painful things being pulled out of my spirit, and with every tug of them being freed, it was replaced with joy I had never felt before. I had so many lies that I had believed for so long, lies that I had allowed to define my worth not only to myself but also in how I viewed my worth to others.

That night began the healing process of God uprooting lies that I had believed well into my childhood. It wasn't always a wonderful feeling, the process, but the peace, the joy I felt on the other side is more than I can put into words.

Allow God room to change that urge to use comparison. Allow God to exchange it for something better. Allow God to use it to push you forward for the plans He has for you. With God by your side, you can accomplish what He has planned for you. You don't have to have the best Christian education or upbringing. You don't have to attend Bible school. You don't have to meet any qualifications anyone else says you have to. You simply have to listen to the voice of God when He calls you and be willing to do what He asks regardless of how insane it may sound at the time.

God can use some of those things I stated above to jumpstart your journey. Bible school is part of what brought this book to life; it can change your life too. If you feel God calling you to attend Bible school, then go for it. If you don't, join a small group that will encourage you and lift you up when the storms of life come around. Make sure that you have some type of support system around you. You can't walk through this life alone.

I remember the night I first started Bible college. The enemy was fighting me *hard* about going to the Bible college offered through my church. I could hear all these lies being thrown my way, and a part of me knew it was the enemy trying to stop me. The enemy told me I wasn't "qualified" to go to Bible college, that I was going to look stupid sitting with people that had been Christians for thirty-plus years. "You don't have what it takes." "You'll look like a fool in front of everyone there." "You'll be left alone." Sitting in the car just outside of the church, I took a moment and prayed. I told God that I was going to give Him one year. One year of Bible college. I told Him that if He didn't change my life around in that one year, I wasn't going back.

The first year of Bible college changed my life in ways I can't even describe. Lies were put under the spotlight and worked out of my life; connections with people in the church were made. While I had gone in thinking that only those that had experience serving in the church deserved to be there, I left realizing that those people that had been in the church for thirty-plus years were learning the same thing as me. They were just as thirsty for God as I was.

It was during that first year that I learned that I didn't have to have my life together before God could use me.

You don't have to have the perfect job, never fight with your husband, be the perfect mom, the perfect roommate, the perfect anything. Let me tell you something: You won't ever be perfect. Even for one day of your life you won't be perfect. You have to put your faith and your trust in God. That's the first step on the right road, a road that will lead you closer to the one who created you.

If you're struggling with the thoughts that you have to be perfect, ask yourself this: If perfection was something we could attain, why would Jesus need to lay His life down for us?

You don't have to be perfect; you don't even have to know what God wants you to do with your life. I still don't. At the time of this book being written, I am a teacher, but I am feeling the tug that my time as such may be coming to an end. I don't know what path God may lead me should I leave child care, but I do know this: Wherever that path leads me, God is right there beside me.

> Trust in the LORD with all your heart And
> do not lean on your own understanding. In all
> your ways acknowledge Him, And He will make
> your paths straight. (Proverbs 3:5–6 NASB)

He is right beside you too. He's walking alongside you; let this scripture be a reminder that the more you focus on Him and lean on His understanding, the more your path will straighten out before you. You may only see one step at a time, but faith takes that step, even when it doesn't see the rest of the steps. Just keep trusting God and putting your focus on Him instead of what the world offers you.

5

You Are Qualified

It is not that we think we are qualified to do anything on our
own. Our qualification comes from God. He has enabled us
to be ministers of his new covenant. This is a covenant not of
written laws, but of the Spirit. The old written covenant ends
in death; but under the new covenant, the Spirit gives life.

—2 Corinthians 3:5–6 (NLT)

In the last chapter, I wrote a little about how we may believe that our
history, our circumstances can disqualify us from being used by God.
Let's dig deeper into this important topic. One thing I have learned
over the years is this: We are not qualified by our own works.

God is the one that qualifies us for His calling on our lives. Isn't
that reassuring? Knowing that no matter how messed up your history might be, God can still qualify you even if the rest of the world
wouldn't can give you such supernatural peace.

I remember my pastor talking about how he would be number
100 if someone was to choose between ten people who would be a
pastor. He was far away from God, wanted nothing to do with God,
but God had other plans for his life.

God didn't take my pastor and spruce him up before setting
him up to be a pastor, no. He started pastoring in his early twenties
and, through his time as a pastor, has impacted countless lives.

His transparency about his history was an inspiration to me
when I was struggling to understand what it meant to be a Christian.

61

He broke down the lie that I'd believed that one had to be perfect in order to be used by God. He spoke about times he had doubted, but how he'd pushed through because he chose to put his faith in God and not in himself.

He is a prime example of how you don't know how many people your testimony might impact. Don't be afraid to allow God to use your muck to reach out to those that are in the same muck you used to be in. God can use your history in the muck, and how He brought you out of it, to give hope to those stuck in the muck themselves.

You don't have to have the best education, the best family history, the best anything to be qualified by God. In fact, He enjoys using those that society has thrown aside and deemed a lost cause. Later on, I'll talk about David, but for now, there is another man in the Bible whose story is also quite powerful. Someone that was seen lowly not only in society but in his family. This man's name was Gideon.

> Then the angel of the Lord came and sat beneath the great tree at Ophrah, which belonged to Joash of the clan of Abiezer. Gideon son of Joash was threshing wheat at the bottom of a winepress to hide the grain from the Midianites. The angel of the Lord appeared to him, and said, "Mighty hero, the Lord is with you!" "Sir," Gideon replied, "if the Lord is with us, why has all this happened to us? And where are all the miracles our ancestors told us about? Didn't they say, 'the Lord brought us up out of Egypt'? But now the Lord has abandoned us and handed us over to the Midianites." The Lord turned to him and said, "Go with the strength you have, and rescue Israel from the Midianites. I am sending you!" "But Lord," Gideon replied, "how can I rescue Israel? My clan is the weakest in the whole tribe of Manasseh, and I am the least in my entire family!" The Lord said to him, "I will be with

you. And you will destroy the Midianites as if you were fighting against one man." (Judges 6:11–16 NLT)

Did you notice how Gideon said "*If* the Lord is with *us*"? The angel had said that the Lord *was* with *him*. Gideon doubted that God was with him when he brought "*if*" into the equation. Gideon doubted that God was with him, let alone those around him. Why? Because of the circumstances surrounding them.

Not only was Gideon focused on the circumstances surrounding himself and his family, but he also pointed out his disqualifications to God: "*My clan is the weakest in the whole tribe…and I am the least in my entire family.*"

Do you think that God cared about Gideon's qualifications when He sent His angel down to speak with Gideon? God already knew Gideon better than Gideon knew himself. Notice, too, that God didn't respond to Gideon's attempts to disqualify himself from the calling He had put on his life. God simply told him, "*I will be with you.*" God is with you too. No matter how much you try to disqualify yourself using your past, your rank, your situations or circumstances, none of that matters to God when He has put a specific calling on your life. He took that all into consideration and called you anyway.

Gideon wasn't the only one that God used that was "underqualified" for the job. Moses; Esther; David; Mary, mother of Jesus; Mary Magdalene; Rahab; Ruth; Jacob; and so many others were disqualified by society for multiple reasons. But God had bigger plans than what society thought these people were capable of. I'll let you in on a little secret: Jesus was underqualified according to those of religious law and those He grew up around as well.

Jesus left that part of the country and returned with his disciples to Nazareth, his hometown. The next Sabbath he began teaching in the synagogue, and many who heard him were amazed. They asked "Where did he get all this

wisdom and the power to perform such miracles?"
Then they scoffed, "He's just a carpenter, the son
of Mary and the brother of James, Joseph, Judas,
and Simon. And his sisters live right here among
us." They were deeply offended and refused to
believe in him. (Mark 6:1–3 NLT)

They were *deeply offended* and *refused to believe in Him*. Wow.
Let that fact sink in for a moment.

Never mind that they had heard of the miracles Jesus had performed and heard what Jesus preached. Jesus didn't meet their level of qualifications for the job he was performing, so instead of applauding him going above his "abilities," they became offended and missed out on an opportunity for God to move in their lives.

There will be people that will be offended by your calling. If it happened to Jesus, it's most likely going to happen to us. There will be those that will attempt to talk you down from the calling God has given you. They may try to come off as helpful by saying such things as "Are you sure you heard God correctly?" "Maybe you should pray on this a little longer before making a decision." "It might not be in your best interest to go down that route." The most well-meaning people can also be the most damaging in our desire to fulfill our calling.

It is important to be sure that your calling is what God has placed on your life by getting input from those around you in authority—your pastor, a mentor, etc. You must also be confident in what God has called you to do. The road will be bumpy at times, and you will fall and scuff your hands and knees, but that's the best position to be in to pray to God for guidance.

When the road gets tough, support from those around you can keep you going when you feel as if your tank is empty. It's important to make sure that those that you allow influence in your life are those that are deeply connected with God.

You don't want to run off the deep end without consulting a trusted person, thinking that you're following God's calling. You also want to make sure that those that are speaking into your life are doing so out of love and not out of any selfish ambition or reasoning.

Having deep, intimate connections with people is vital to our growth not only as people but also as Christians. There is a woman I know who is living this truth continually in her life. She is raising three children while caring for her husband after he was injured in a horrible accident. Her story is one filled with encouragement, determination, dedication, hope, and unconditional love.

Shannon is one of the most inspirational stories I've heard when I began to interview people for this book. When I first met her many years ago, I thought that she must've had a wonderful upbringing to be able to be an essentially walking sunshine.

She radiates Jesus and has such a heart for people. She loves with everything that is in her, and she makes those around her feel welcomed and accepted regardless of their history.

It was during a small group with my church that I first heard her story. Shannon spoke of how her upbringing hadn't been a good one. When she was growing up, her family did not have running water or electricity, and her family tended to live off of the land. She said her parents lived the "hippy" type of lifestyle.

When her parents divorced, they had a negative view on each other and didn't speak to each other. If they had something to say to the other parent, it was done through the children.

Her mother ended up marrying a man while he was still in jail, and once he was out of jail, he beat on her. When her mother had told Shannon to call the police one night, he ripped the phone line out of the wall, and she had to leave the house and go to a payphone to call the police.

This wasn't the end of her mother's rough road, sadly. Her mother ended up getting into hard drugs, and due to that, Shannon and her siblings would have their water and electricity turned off. Eventually, her mother left the state leaving the children—Shannon included—to fend for themselves.

Shannon was lucky enough that her siblings were able to take her in as she was too young to care for herself. She had to couch surf for some time while she was in high school on top of looking for a job at fourteen years old to provide for herself. Due to this dysfunctional upbringing and the people she hung around with, Shannon got into weed and alcohol at a young age.

Sometime later, there was a friend that invited her to church, and during that time, Shannon changed and wholeheartedly went after God. Sadly, the things of this world began to overshadow the passion she felt for God, and she began to grow distant from Him. She loved Him, but the trials of life pulled her attention away. One of her sisters moved back into the state, and when she did, she got Shannon to go with her to church.

At first, Shannon told me she struggled to feel the presence of God. She would lift her hands and praise God, but not feel anything different when she did. During a visit to Faith Center Church for a youth event, Shannon was given the chance to get baptized. This was where things shifted for her. She explained to me that everything from her past just melted away in the water, and she chose to turn her life around.

This change didn't mean her struggles were over yet. Years passed, and she got married. She and her husband had to stand in agreement and fight when they struggled with getting pregnant. When they did get pregnant, they were told that their child had signs that she was going to be born with Down syndrome. Shannon told me this was the first tangible moment that she was able to see her faith come through. She and her husband agreed that they were going to pray for their child using scriptures regardless of what the doctors told her about their child. Her eldest was born healthy, and she has since had two other children.

The biggest part of Shannon's testimony came with the car accident that threw her world upside down. This part of the story starts with it being the middle of the night when she felt a tug that told her to check her phone. When she did, she realized she had missed a call from the hospital. When she called them back, she found out that her husband had been in a motorcycle accident. The accident was severe. He was lucky to be alive. His injuries varied from broken bones to skull fragments embedded in his brain.

The doctors didn't give her much hope when it came to his diagnosis. While she could have chosen to give up on her husband

and whatever future she had planned for the two of them, Shannon didn't. Instead, she chose to praise God through it by singing songs while sitting next to her husband in the hospital. Her faith was in God, and He was her firm foundation. At the time of the accident, Shannon was also heavily pregnant with their third child.

Now, not only did she have to care for her two daughters as well as the child inside of her, but she had to care for her husband as well. Thankfully, the church pulled together and surrounded her with support. People from the church would not only bring her meals to take care of herself and her husband but would also offer support to her emotionally and financially as well. She explained it felt like such a blessing to have so many people come together to support her and her family.

Over the years, her husband has recovered above and beyond what the doctors ever anticipated he would. While he still needs constant care, and he still has a long way to go, Shannon is still holding strong to her faith that her husband will be healed and she praises God for his progress. She is teaching her children to do the same. Her sweet daughters were my late niece's best friends. They have overcome a lot in their young life and have a passion for others and for God. Their mother is one of the most inspirational people I know.

After learning about Shannon's history, I was shocked. She had gone through so much in her life and still was so dedicated to God. Part of me wondered how she could stay so faithful when going through everything she had. Shannon told me the importance of scripture when it came to overcoming these times. That focusing on God's Word is the best course of action when these types of times arise.

Our emotions are fickle and change often; whereas the Bible is the same yesterday, today, and always. God and His love for us will never change. God has given us His word to help us through we need only to put our hope and trust in Him.

> The name of the Lord is a strong fortress;
> the godly run to him and are safe. (Proverbs
> 18:10 NLT)

I mentioned earlier how at times we look at someone and assume that they've had an amazing Christian upbringing, that they haven't had to go through struggles like we have. We assume things about others without knowing even a fraction of their story. The sad part is when we disqualify ourselves based off of that assumption. We won't know the entire history of everyone we meet, and assuming we know based off their current location in life will only drag us deeper into the darkness of shame.

When we go through hardships in our lives, many times we want to know and understand everything before we are willing to believe that we will make it through it. We want to see God's plan so we can "approve" before He implements it. That's not faith. Faith is belief without sight. Sometimes these times when we can't see the entire road before us are what deepen our faith in God. This is where the roots of our faith dig in deep making it so we can weather the storms that come.

> Consider it nothing but joy, my brothers and sisters, whenever you fall into various trials. Be assured that the testing of your faith [through experience] produces endurance [leading to spiritual maturity, and inner peace]. (James 1:2–3 AMP)

Trials give us a chance to run the race of endurance. Remember, it's not by our strength that we are able to run this race, but with Jesus, we can run the race and finish strong. I heard a sermon years ago that spoke about how a seed cannot grow unless it is planted. The seed must be put into the ground, but in order for it to thrive, it must push through the dirt in order to bloom.

As Christians, we are on the same journey. Heaven is where we will reach the end of our race, but while we're here on earth, we can use our hardships to encourage others to keep fighting the good fight!

> We can rejoice, too, when we run into problems and trials, for we know that they will help

> us develop endurance. And endurance develops
> strength of character, and character strengthens
> our confident hope of salvation. And this hope
> will not lead to disappointment. For we know
> how dearly God loves us, because he has given
> us the Holy Spirit to fill our hearts with his love.
> (Romans 5:3–5 NLT)

> Fight the good fight for the true faith. Hold
> tightly to the eternal life to which God has called
> you, which you have declared so well before
> many witnesses. (1 Timothy 6:12 NLT)

The Bible is filled with people who fought the fight of faith. Those that had to look at their circumstances in their life and believe God's Word over what they saw with their eyes. Remember, there were those that doubted, though; you're not the only one. They made the choice to push past their doubt and believe. You have the choice to do the same.

Their stories are meant to encourage us to follow the same path they did, to put our faith in the One that created the heavens and the earth. You are called by God. You have a unique and specific calling on your life.

When we believe that our past disqualifies us from God using us, it will keep us from fulfilling the plans and purpose that God has for our lives. It's a lie from the enemy we have to fight, sometimes daily, but it's during that fight that we become stronger by relying on the Word of God to define us.

> But now your kingdom must end, for the
> Lord has sought out a man after his own heart.
> The Lord has already appointed him to be the
> leader of his people, because you have not kept
> the Lord's command. (1 Samuel 13:14 NLT)

This scripture is talking about David. Many of us know the story of how he slayed Goliath, and the scripture says that David was a man "after God's own heart." One very important thing to remember about David though is that he messed up. David sinned. He was just as human as the rest of us, but those sins he committed did not strip away the title of "man after God's own heart" from him.

David committed adultery with a woman named Bathsheba; and when she became pregnant, he had her husband, Uriah, killed on the battlefield so as to hide his adultery with the woman. David wasn't disqualified because of his choices; he had to deal with the consequences that arose from such, but God didn't abandon him or His calling on David's life because of the them.

The mistakes you've made over your lifetime, no matter how far back or recent they may be, will never be enough to disrupt the calling that God has for your life. The peace that accompanies the knowledge of how God sees us is unlike anything this world can offer. Allow God to redefine your identity. Allow God to show you how He sees you and welcome that revelation from Him.

6

There Is Hope in the Dark

Purify me from my sins, and I will be clean;
wash me, and I will be whiter than snow.
—Psalm 51:7 (NLT)

One important thing to remember during this journey with God is that it is just that: a journey. I've touched on this subject quite a few times during the book, but if you're anything like I am, repetitiveness sometimes is what's needed to get those important details into our brain.

We have to overcome old habits and lifestyles that once held us back. Just as a caterpillar doesn't become a butterfly overnight, we don't always suddenly overcome our former addictions or lifestyles.

I was reading a book to a toddler while at work, and one of the books talked about was how we need to be patient when things don't happen in the time frame we want them to. It was a simple book, but it was impactful in that moment. It was a little reminder that it is okay for things to develop over time.

There have been some people that have been able to leave their old life almost overnight; while for others, it has taken years. There is no shame in this. I won't say that those that broke their old habits overnight had "more faith" than those that took years to overcome theirs. It's not the truth. I cannot explain why some are freed quickly while for others, it takes time.

Remember to extend grace to yourself while you're learning to become who God created you to be. Before you know it, you will look back and see you've come a lot farther than you ever thought you could. It begins with the desire to change and realize you need help doing so.

> Well then, since God's grace has set us free from the law, does that mean we can go on sinning? Of course not! Don't you realize that you become the slave of whatever you choose to obey? You can be a slave to sin, which leads to death, or you can choose to obey God, which leads to righteous living. Thank God! Once you were slaves of sin but now you wholehearted obey this teaching we have given you. Now you are free from your slavery to sin, and you have become slaves to righteous living. (Romans 6:15–18 NLT)

We have a choice. God will not force His love on us, nor will He force us to take the right path. He won't force righteous living on those that wish to continue living in sin. He has given us free will, but even in that free will, we are not free of the consequences that can come by way of that.

I want to clarify something before we continue: There is a difference between *living* in sin and *committing* a sin. I touched on this a little before with the woman caught in adultery. We all sin. Daily. No matter if we've been a Christian for a week or for sixty years. We all fall short, which is why we need God's help and Jesus's sacrifice.

Though we may commit a sin, we should be striving to grow closer to God. When we do sin, we feel remorse and want to change our ways. We don't want to continue to walk in that path.

As Christians we strive to sin less, and we do get a little better each day. We sin less than those that live in the world. We sin less because we are striving to please God with our actions; whereas the world doesn't care if their actions please God or not.

Living in sin is knowing that something is a sin; and willfully doing it anyways on a continual basis, unrepentant, it becomes a choice that we simply ignored, and there is no problem found with living that way. When living in sin, one don't feel guilt or a desire to change their behavior or actions.

An example I will use is having sex before marriage: One who is living in sin will continue to have sex with their partner even after accepting Jesus as their savior. This person isn't beyond redemption, but they need to recognize that what they are doing isn't a part of God's plan for their life. If this lifestyle continues, it will draw them away from God instead of drawing them closer to God.

Living in sin does not coincide with living with the Holy Spirit inside of you. This is simply due to the fact that sin separates us from God. Living a life of sin and having the Holy Spirit within you is not something that can be done. The Holy Spirit's job is to convict us of sin, not to encourage us to continue in a sinful lifestyle.

One who used to have sex with their partner before and chooses to do so no longer is repentant for their actions; they are making the choice to change their actions and strive to draw closer to God despite their weaknesses. They chose this route instead of justifying or excusing their former behavior even if their flesh still wants to live in that particular sin.

This was a lesson I had to learn the hard way during my addiction with pornography and masturbation. I wrote earlier about how I was introduced to sex at a young age; that was the gateway that was opened, and because I didn't address what had happened with anyone else, it left that door open. That would end up with an addiction that took over a good amount of my life.

At this time of my life, I still struggled with masturbation as I assumed I wasn't having sex with anyone else, so I didn't think it was that big of a deal. I managed to keep it hidden from my parents and didn't realize just how much of a hold it had on me until that hold became stronger. When I was around twelve years old, I was in an online chatroom. I didn't think much of it; I was just talking with people about random stuff twelve-year-olds do. I was speaking to a lady who asked me if I'd ever watched pornography. I didn't know what it was at that time so I told her "no." It was then she sent me a link to a website that introduced me to one of the most lengthy and difficult struggles of my life.

This was around the same time I had started attending church again and was just realizing that God didn't hate me for what had happened when I was five. I was just starting to realize there was hope in the darkness I'd been stuck in for so long.

I was curious and followed the link. It was there I was exposed to sex on demand, and I quickly became hooked. I also kept this a secret from my family and suffered in silence. My view of sex was still skewed, and I didn't understand how addicting pornography could become.

I quickly began to watch it almost on a daily basis. I justified what I was doing even when I was ashamed when I participated in it. Pornography became an added addiction that grew in the darkness of my secrecy.

There is almost always a reason behind the addiction—some emotion one is trying to flee from to find relief from. For me, I fell into pornography and self-pleasure as well as inappropriate online roleplaying due to the emotions I was struggling with at the time.

I felt invisible in day-to-day life. I didn't feel known, wanted, or celebrated. So instead of addressing that pain, I decided to run, to use an escape to hide the pain in the hopes that it would go away.

Perhaps it was because I was exposed to sex at such a young age, and the pleasure was something temporary that would make me feel better and help me forget about my life if only for a moment. At that age, fantasy was a normal thing for a child to get lost in, which also hindered my ability to address my issues. Fantasy became an escape from the negative emotions I would feel, and over time, I became conditioned to run to it instead of God.

When I felt like I had little to no control over the situations and circumstances in my life, I would turn to something I could control: my online roleplays and my sexual activity. In my roleplays, I could become whomever I wanted and join whatever created world I wished. I could control how people responded to me, and I didn't have to worry about rejection. I could leave my glasses-wearing, overweight, low-self-esteem, bookworm self behind and be someone I saw as more valuable than the real me.

It became easy over the years to run to this "solution" when things got difficult. I didn't even realize how deep in the darkness I was until I wanted to be free and wanted to get closer to God. I didn't want this sin to hold me back from what He had for my life any longer.

Over time, I ended up at a different church than the one I got saved in; another friend invited me to her church, and I have been attending there ever since. It was a few years after I was introduced to pornography, and she invited me to join her at a purity conference. I attended, and while I was given an understanding that what I was doing, the pornography and self-pleasure, was wrong, I wasn't condemned like I had been all those years ago. Instead, I was given hope that with Jesus I could overcome this temptation—that I wasn't alone. That was the beginning of hope in my life that I could be free, that God would help me overcome this struggle. At the time, I thought it would be as quick as snapping my fingers; little did I know just how wrong I was.

A part of me wanted to be free of this, to finally feel the chains off of my wrists, I just didn't know where to begin. Some scripture still scared me, as I didn't understand the meaning behind grace and that Jesus died for my past, present, *and* future sins. I didn't understand that Jesus *already saw* our future sins and nailed those to the cross as well. I thought any sin that you committed *after* Jesus saved you meant you had to repent and start all over again.

> We are made right with God by placing our faith in Jesus Christ. And this is true for everyone who believes, no matter who we are. For everyone has sinned; we all fall short of God's glorious standard. Yet God, in his grace, freely makes us right in his sight. He did this through Christ Jesus when he freed us from the penalty for our sins. (Romans 3:22–24 NLT)

The Amplified version goes a little deeper: "[All] are justified and made upright and in right standing with God, freely and gratuitously by His grace [His unmerited favor and mercy], through the redemption which is (provided) in Christ Jesus."

We all fall short. The only perfect human being was Jesus. This is something that I wish I could say was an easy thing to understand. I believe more people struggle with this than we realize. We don't vocalize our struggles with our understanding of scripture because we don't want to be told to "figure it out" or feel ashamed or even stupid for asking.

Let me assure you the fact that you struggle with sin daily doesn't mean there's something wrong with you. It means you're human. That being said, you can't give up on the fight to be more like Jesus.

Remember when I talked about how powerful our testimonies can be when it comes to helping others? By sharing our testimonies, we are telling others that we're not perfect, that God doesn't expect us to be perfect, that we're on the same journey and they're just as loved as we are, that they are accepted by Jesus just as they are. They don't have to "clean up" before coming to Him.

This truth is more powerful than we realize. This truth, especially when shared with the testimony about what God has brought you through offers hope, encouragement, and freedom to those still in bondage and believing the lies of the enemy.

It's not only other Christians who can add to the bondage by using scripture and twisting it. For the longest time, the devil twisted scriptures in my mind to dig me deeper into bondage. Scriptures like:

> God's will is for you to be holy, so stay away
> from sexual sin. Then each of you will control his
> own body and live in holiness and honor—not in
> lustful passion like the pagans who do not know
> God and his ways. (1 Thessalonians 4:3–5 NLT)

> When you follow the desires of your sinful
> nature, the results are very clear: Sexual immo-
> rality, lustful pleasures, idolatry, sorcery, hostility,

> quarreling, jealousy, outbursts of anger, selfish ambition, dissension, division, envy, drunkenness, wild partis, and other sins like these. Let me tell you again, as I have before, that anyone living that sort of life will not inherit the Kingdom of God. (Galatians 5:19–21 NLT)

> Don't you realize that those who do wrong will not inherit the Kingdom of God? Don't fool yourselves. Those who indulge in sexual sin, or who worship idols, or commit adultery, or are male prostitutes, or practice homosexuality, or are thieves, or greedy people, or drunkards, or are abusive, or cheat people-none of these will inherit the Kingdom of God. (1 Corinthians 6:9–10 NLT)

That last scripture terrified me for a long time. The devil used it to keep me bound up and keep me from running *to* God when I needed Him most. The devil would tell me, "God doesn't want anything to do with you." "You call yourself a Christian and you fall into pornography almost on a daily basis." "You can't be used by God." All these lies and more would repeat in my head over and over again until I felt paralyzed.

Even though I knew Jesus loved me and forgave me, I was sure that God could never use me, that I would never be with Him because I struggled with sin after being born again. The devil made me believe that you had to be perfect in order to be truly saved, that if I struggled with sin, especially sexual sin, that I was beyond helping, beyond hope.

This lie was one that also almost led me to hurting myself many times. I had thoughts of cutting my wrist or taking a bottle of pills. I didn't think there was hope that my life would get any better. I felt that I was stuck in this vicious cycle with no way to be free.

I would feel condemnation whenever communion was served in the church, but I still had a glimmer of hope in my spirit that God would look upon me and show compassion toward me, see that I was trying to get better, trying to break free of my old habit. I thought I had to perform in order to "earn" His love.

These warnings in the Bible are meant to guide us away from the lifestyles the world deems as "appropriate" or "approved." We are not to be conformed or live in the ways of this world, but we are to be transformed by the renewing of our minds. To renew our minds, we must focus on something different. We can't be renewed if we're living in the same gunk that we're trying to get out of. We can renew our minds by focusing on God, drawing close to him—whether that be through Bible reading, listening to an audiobook, talking to a mentor, or listening to worship music.

The Amplified goes deeper into these scriptures to aid our understanding:

> For you know what commandments and precepts we gave you by the authority of the Lord Jesus. For this is the will of God, that you be sanctified [separated and set apart from sin]: that you abstain and back away from sexual immorality; that each of you know how to control his own body in holiness and honor [being available for God's purpose and separated from things profane]. (1 Thessalonians 4:2–4 AMP)

> Now the practices of the sinful nature are clearly evident: they are sexual immorality, impurity, sensuality (total irresponsibility, lack of self-control), idolatry, sorcery, hostility, strife, jealousy, fits of anger, disputes, dissensions, factions [that promote heresies], envy, drunkenness, riotous behavior, and other things like these. I warn you beforehand, just as I did previously, that those who practice such things will not inherit the kingdom of God. (Galatians 5:19–21 AMP)

> Do you not know that the unrighteous will not inherit or have any share in the kingdom of God? Do not be deceived; neither the sexually immoral, nor idolaters, nor adulterers, nor effeminate [by perversion], nor those who participate in homosexuality, nor thieves, nor the greedy, nor drunkards, nor revilers [whose words are used as weapons to abuse, insult, humiliate, intimidate, or slander], nor swindlers will inherit or have any share in the kingdom of God. (1 Corinthians 6:9–10 AMP)

I'm going to add one more verse in that particular scripture that I wish I had read when I read that last verse so many years ago:

> And such some of you were (once). But you were washed clean (purified by a complete atonement for sin and made free from the guilt of sin); and you were consecrated (set apart, hallowed); and you were justified (pronounced righteous, by trust) in the name of the Lord Jesus Christ and in the (Holy) Spirit of our God.
>
> So if the Son sets you free, you are truly free. (John 8:36 NLT)

> "I, the Lord, have called you to demonstrate my righteousness. I will take you by the hand and guard you, and I will give you to my people, Israel, as a symbol of my covenant with them. And you will be a light to guide the nations. You will open the eyes of the blind. You will free the captives from prison, releasing those who sit in dark dungeons." (Isaiah 42:6–7 NLT)

The scripture above is talking about Jesus, but we are to be Christlike. You are no longer a prisoner, dear one. You are set free by the actions of Jesus dying on the cross for you. He didn't do it expecting you to be perfect; He did it because He loves you. His love is everlasting and unconditional! Often we get caught up in remembering the times we have fallen and how badly we screw up. God doesn't. Once we repent, it is forgotten. We and the devil are the ones who remember, and the devil would love nothing more than for us to dwell on our shortcomings instead of focusing on how far God's brought us and the amazing plans that He has for our life. We need only rely on His guidance and support.

> "Come now, let's settle this," says the Lord. "Though your sins are like scarlet, I will make them as white as snow. Though they are red like crimson, I will make them as white as wool." (Isaiah 1:18 NLT)

There are times it's difficult to believe that our sins are gone, that God sees us as white as snow. When we look at ourselves, we can see the labels that others have placed on us, or we have placed on ourselves: sinner, unworthy, unloved, unwanted, broken, addicted, overweight/fat, underweight/skinny, nerd—fill in the labels you've had put on you or you have put on yourself. We all have them, but we have a choice on whether we allow them to define who we are. I'll talk more about labels and how they hinder how we believe God views us in the next chapter.

King David had many labels put on him. We don't know much about his history, but we do know that his father didn't include him when he was told to present his sons, which is pretty harsh. It was only after all seven of his father's sons were rejected was David even brought up. Do you relate to David? Do you feel that those around you don't recognize you as a part of their "family" or "group"? There is hope if you do. Read on what God says about David.

> When they arrived, Samuel took one look at Eliab and thought, "Surely this is the Lord's anointed!" But the Lord said to Samuel, "Don't

judge by his appearance or height, for I have rejected him. The Lord doesn't see things the way you see them. People judge by outward appearances but the Lord looks at the heart. Then Jesse told his son Abinadab to step forward and walk in front of Samuel. But Samuel said, "This is not the one the Lord has chosen." Next Jesse summoned Shimea, but Samuel said, "Neither is this one the Lord has chosen." In the same way all seven of Jesse's sons were presented to Samuel. But Samuel said to Jesse, "The Lord has not chosen any of these." Then Samuel asked, "Are these all the sons you have?" "There is still the youngest," Jesse replied. "But he's out in the field watching the sheep and goats." "Send for him at once." Samuel said. "We will not sit down to eat until he arrives." So Jesse sent for him. He was dark and handsome, with beautiful eyes. And the Lord said, "This is the one, anoint him." (1 Samuel 16:6–12 NLT)

It can feel like it's near impossible to rid ourselves of the labels on us, especially if they were enforced at a young age or by those we deeply respect or love. The guilt that can come with those labels can make it all the more difficult to fight them. This is why it's so important to know that God's thoughts are vastly different from our own thoughts. His thoughts of us are higher than the ones we think up ourselves.

We can be so focused on achieving salvation, healing, or breakthrough by our own words or actions that we forget that all of that is a gift from God.

Can we boast, then, that we have done anything to be accepted by God? No, because our acquittal is not based on obeying the law. It is based on faith. So we are made right with

God through faith and not by obeying the law.
(Romans 3:27–28 NLT)

But people were counted as righteous, not
because of their work, but because of their faith
in God who forgives sinners. (Romans 4:5 NLT)

Let me clarify something before we continue on; the law was and is good. The law is of God, and since God is good, the law is good as well. The point of the law is to point us to the fact that we *cannot* fulfill the law on our own. At some point, in every single day of our lives, we will fail in some way or another; if not physically then mentally. We need someone, a savior, who can achieve what we cannot. That was Jesus.

Another reason I believe the law was put into place and why we can't *earn* our salvation or gifts from God is because we would fall into pride. Who can say that they haven't been prideful in something they accomplished? You see, I don't think pride in and of itself is sinful. It's okay to be proud of your achievements; it's when those accomplishments or achievements become a part of your identity that you fall into trouble. Your identity *must* come from God.

7

Identity and Faith

For I am not ashamed of this Good News about Christ. It is the power of God at work saving everyone who believes-the Jew first and also the Gentile. This Good News tells us how God makes us right in his sight. This is accomplished from start to finish by faith. As the scriptures say, "It is through faith that a righteous person has life."

—Romans 1:16–17 (NLT)

When we accept Jesus as our savior our identity changes. From someone that is away from God, disconnected, we become someone that is welcomed with open arms regardless of our sins. This may be difficult for you to understand, as so often, we feel that we have to *earn* our acceptance from God. That we have to meet some standard in order to be acceptable to Him.

The amazing thing is that this isn't true. If you allow yourself to believe that God loves you while knowing every bit of your past, the parts of yourself you're ashamed of, knowing every mistake and sin, every choice, every kind or harsh word said to another or to yourself, you will be set free.

You don't have to strive in order to have God accept you. You don't have to get your life together before you go to Him. That's truly an amazing thing! God isn't looking to punish you for all that you've done. He wants to welcome you home with open arms.

"In the same way, there is joy in the presence of God's angels when even one sinner repents." To illustrate the point further, Jesus told them this story: "A man had two sons. The younger son told his father, 'I want my share of your estate now before you die.' So his father agreed to divide his wealth between his sons. A few days later this younger son packed all his belongings and moved to a distant land, and there he wasted all his money in wild living. About the time his money ran out, a great famine swept over the land, and he began to starve. He persuaded a local farmer to hire him into his fields to feed the pigs. The young man became so hungry that even the pods he was feeding the pigs looked good to him. But no one gave him anything.

When he finally came to his senses, he said to himself. 'At home even the hired servants have food enough to spare, and here I am dying of hunger! I will go home to my father and say, "Father, I have sinned against both heaven and you, I am no longer worthy of being called your son. Please take me on as a hired servant."' So he returned home to his father. And while he was still a long way off his father saw him coming. Filled with love and compassion, he ran to his son, embraced him, and kissed him. His son said to him, "Father, I have sinned against both heaven and you, and I am no longer worthy of being called your son." But his father said to the servants, "Quick! Bring the finest robe in the house and put it on him. Get a ring for his finger and sandals for his feet. And kill the calf we have been fattening. We must celebrate with a feast, for this son of mine was dead and has returned

to life. He was lost, but now he is found." So the
party began. (Luke 15:10–24 NLT)

When we live unrepentant lives away from God, as the son in
this story did, our spirit is dead. When we return to God, as the son
returned home to his father, we are brought back to life. Notice that
the father didn't ask what his son's sins had been. He didn't ask where
the money he'd given him had gone or what he had spent it on. He
wasn't even angry with his son for leaving the way that he had. The
way this father welcomed his son home with open arms is the same
way God welcomes us home when we return to him.

We can struggle with truly believing that's how God responds
to us coming home. We may have had bad examples for parents or
no parents who raised us at all. However, the fact that God created
us backs up this scripture. He didn't create us by mistake. Not one
person is ever born a mistake. Including you.

For many years, I felt like I was a mistake. In part due to the fact
that my family is a blended family, I felt like I was the child from the
broken marriage. I thought I was a mistake, that I was an outcast. I
never voiced this to my parents for fear that they would confirm this.
With God, there is no reason to fear how He feels about you. He
makes it clear in Scripture just how much He loves you.

We are His children, and He rejoices when we return home to
Him. He will not ask us to list everything we've done wrong. We
don't have to clean ourselves up before we can return to Him. That's
the beauty of grace!

God is love. That is truth. God is our Father. That is also truth.
For some people understanding that God is a *loving* Father is difficult for them. Some never knew their earthly fathers or lost them
some time early in their life. Others watched their fathers struggle
with addiction or choices in their life that negatively impacted them.
Sadly, there are even those that have suffered from abuse by the hand
of their earthly father. For those that have struggled in their relationship with their fathers, it can be difficult to understand how our
heavenly father could be any different.

Scriptures that may help this comprehension of God and His love for us are ones similar to these below:

> But God clearly shows and proves His own love for us, by the fact that while we were still sinners, Christ died for us. (Romans 5:8 AMP)

> But God, being (so very) rich in mercy, because of His great and wonderful love with which He loved us, even when we were (spiritually) dead and separated from Him because of our sins, He made us (spiritually) alive together with Christ (for by His grace His undeserved favor and mercy-you have been saved from God's judgement). (Ephesians 2:4–5 AMP)

> Beloved, let us (unselfishly) love and seek the best for one another, for love is from God; and everyone who loves (others) is born of God and knows God (through personal experience). The one who does not love has not become acquainted with God (does not and never did know Him), for God is love. (He is the originator of love, and it is an enduring attribute of his nature.) (1 John 4:7–8 AMP)

> The Lord appeared to me (Israel) from ages past, saying, "I have loved you with an everlasting love; therefore with lovingkindness I have drawn you and continued my faithfulness to you." (Jeremiah 31:3 AMP)

> There is no fear in love (dread does not exist). But perfect (complete, full-grown) love drives out fear, because fear involves (the expectation of divine) punishment, so the one who

is afraid (Of God's judgement) is not perfected
in love (has not grown into a sufficient understanding of God's love). We love, because He first
loved us. (1 John 4:18–19)

The last scripture hit me rather deeply during my journey with
God. I love my biological father as well as my stepfather, but there are
things I wished that were better between us. Neither of my fathers are
emotional men, at least around me. There were times I wondered if
they were proud of me. I longed to know I mattered to them, to know
that I have a place in their heart. Now, I *know* that they love me, but
there's something about *hearing* your father—or a man in your life
that is a father figure to you- say those precious things to you.

If you were raised in a dysfunctional family, I want you to know
there is hope. God invites us to be a part of His family.

There is no striving for His love, no wondering if He truly cares,
no fear of Him walking away when He sees the mess we are under the
mask we try to hold up. God's love is assured for you, for me, for all
who seek Him wholeheartedly.

We can come to God covered in dirt, hungry, tired, lost, just
as the son in this parable did. It's our choice to return to Him. He
is saddened by those that choose not to return to Him and by those
that deny His very existence. His love is still there for them, but grace
is a gift that one must accept. He won't force Himself on those that
don't wish to have a relationship with Him.

For the wages of sin is death, but the free
gift of God is eternal life through Christ Jesus our
Lord. (Romans 6:23 NLT)

God has given us a gift through Jesus! For a gift to be received,
however, it has to be accepted. We have to accept Jesus in order to
have eternal life with God. It's as simple as that. Acceptance is where
our eternal journey begins.

The Spirit alone gives eternal life. Human effort accomplishes nothing. And the very words I have spoken to you are spirit and life. (John 6:63 NLT)

For this is how God loved the world: he gave his one and only Son, so that everyone who believed in him will not perish but have eternal life. God sent his Son into the world not to judge the world, but to save the world through him. There is no judgement against anyone who believes in him. But anyone who does not believe in him has already been judged for not believing in God's one and only Son. And the judgment is based on this fact: God's light came into the world, but people loved the darkness more than the light, for their actions were evil. All who do evil hate the light and refuse to go near it for fear their sins will be exposed. But those who do what is right come to the light so others can see that they are obeying what God wants. (John 3:16–21 NLT)

This can be a lot to take in, but the choice is ours. We can choose to love the darkness, our sins more than we love God's light, or we can choose to let God's light shine on our sins so we can truly be free from our all of the stuff that weighed us down before. None of it is too big for God to overcome. Nowhere in the Bible does it say that God has a limit on how many sins He's willing to forgive. If you've been told otherwise, it is a lie the devil likes to use to try and keep us from drawing closer to God. If he can prevent us from going to God thinking we have to be perfect then he wins. Don't let him win.

Seek the Lord while you can find him. Call on him now while he is near. Let the wicked change their ways and banish the very thought of

doing wrong. Let them turn to the Lord that he
may have mercy on them. Yes, turn to our God,
for he will forgive generously. (Isaiah 55:6–7
NLT)

I—Yes, I alone—will blot out your sins for
my own sake and will never think of them again.
(Isaiah 43:25 NLT)

He has removed our sins as far from us as
the East is from the West. (Psalm 103:12 NLT)

We can and will have victory. Not by our might or by our power, but by the might and power of Christ in us. Jesus worked miracles on those that society had cast aside. Jesus banished demons from possessed people. He healed those that society had cast out for medical problems they had or choices they made in their life. Jesus can work a miracle in you as well. He can heal you of your past. He can and will give you a hope and a future. It will happen; you can't give up. The journey helps build our faith and make it stronger. Each step makes an impact in our lives and the lives around us.

One of the most inspirational stories I heard over the years came from my own church. Nicole was born four months prematurely, weighing the same amount as a soup can. Doctors gave her a 10 percent chance of survival and a 5 percent chance of having cognitive functioning.

God was faithful and provided many miracles as her parents and many others prayed and spoke the promises of God over her. Her mother told me how they had prayer and scripture recorded and would play it near the incubator Nicole was in when she or her husband weren't able to be there.

There were a lot of medical issues she had to overcome. One of them was cerebral palsy. Her parents trusted that she would be healed, and when she was fourteen she started to engage in fighting for her healing for herself.

After six years of saying scriptures and speaking to her mountain instead of relying on others to speak to it for her, as well as doing things in the natural to help, doctors declared they couldn't find any signs of cerebral palsy other than the scars that she had. She credits her healing to God.

When I asked Nicole what the hardest part of this whole ordeal was—and she had to go through many surgeries over the years to get to the point of healing—she told me,

> Honestly, the hardest part was being made fun of by kids who didn't understand how to treat someone who was different from them. I had many Christian peers and adults discourage me in my fight for healing because they said it was impossible, I must be sinning to be so sick, or that God was trying to teach me a lesson. These comments from religious leaders really messed with me because they were in positions I was supposed to respect, yet I had to challenge and stand up to them.

The enemy loves to use lies to try and get us off track. I asked Nicole what some of the lies she heard during this time:

> So many! The main one being that I was crazy for trusting and believing for healing from a diagnosis that is irreversible. The devil would put thoughts in my head that I was just lying when I said I was healed (speaking the Word) and still in pain, wheelchairs, walkers, etc. However, as I remained consistent, the truth of God's promises outlived every lie of the devil.

Nicole told me two Scriptures that she held onto and used during her situation and during her time of waiting:

> Philippians 1:6 is my life verse that my parents spoke over me from day one and I continue to: *I am confident of this very thing: that He who began a good work in you will be faithful to complete it until the day of Christ Jesus.*
>
> "He himself bore our iniquities in his body on the tree, that we might die to sin and live to righteousness. By his wounds you have been healed" (1 Peter 2:24).

Nicole has since run a marathon, she's an elementary school teacher, and she shows no signs of her former illness. Her story was one that shook me to my core when I heard it. If this family, if this young woman could have such strong faith that she overcame something as severe as cerebral palsy, I could do the same. I had to keep drawing closer to God and allow my faith to grow deeper roots even in the time of waiting. Nicole continues to share her testimony with others and in doing so encourages many to fight their own fight of faith.

> Then Jesus said to the disciples, "Have faith in God. I tell you the truth, you can say to this mountain, 'May you be lifted up and thrown into the sea,' and it will happen. But you must really believe it will happen and have no doubt in your heart. I tell you, you can pray for anything, and if you believe that you've received it, it will be yours. But when you are praying, first forgive anyone you are holding a grudge against, so that your Father in heaven will forgive your sins, too."
> (Mark 11:22–26 NLT)

At times the mountains may be moved in a day, such as with the woman with the issue of blood, the lepers and those that Jesus raised from the dead. Other times, it takes time for those things to come to pass, for the circumstances of life to line up with the Word of God. Do not give up if you do not receive what you've asked for after the first day! With every day that passes, that is another stone from that mountain being moved. Keep moving! Do not give up just because you don't see the results that you want on your timeline.

I recently heard during a church service, "Your faith will always seem smaller than your circumstances." This is true. Anyone who has gone through any hardship in their life will tell you that they felt like it was a monumental task to overcome this situation or circumstance.

God doesn't need big faith to move, though. You don't have to be a pastor, a speaker, or an author. You are a child of God; He needs faith. Not faith in ourselves and our abilities to move that mountain, but faith in Him to move that mountain.

> Pray in the Spirit at all times and on every occasion. Stay alert and be persistent in your prayers for all believers everywhere. (Ephesians 6:18 NLT)

> So let's not get tired of doing what is good. At just the right time we will reap a harvest of blessings if we don't give up. (Galatians 6:9 NLT)

In 2020, a pandemic swept through the world. I won't get into details as everyone has their own opinion about it, but one of the facts is that many places were locked down, and some closed for good.

At the time, I was working as a child care teacher in a Christian daycare. One Friday, March 13, we said goodbye to the students as they headed home, not knowing that it would be the last time we would see some of them. My center was closed for a week while they decided what they were going to do. During this time, I believed that God would provide and wasn't worried about work. In fact, I was going stir crazy by the end of the week and was ready to get back into my classroom.

The numbers were low for our center for a long time, low enough that a coworker of mine and I combined our rooms together. This gave us a chance to talk and encourage each other through this uncertain time.

Due to our center having low numbers, my boss was concerned if we would be able to make it through the summer. Being a non-profit was especially difficult at this time. Summer numbers were always lower anyway due to families going on vacation or teachers pulling their kids out for the summer since they weren't working. My coworker and I didn't worry about it much; instead, we agreed to pray about the daycare and stand in the belief that we would make it through somehow.

Months went on, our numbers were still low. For a nonprofit daycare, this was devastating; it could be the difference between squeaking by and closing the doors. At this time, there were larger state-funded daycares that were shutting down. My coworker and I believed that our daycare would make it through somehow. Even when circumstances seemed at their worst, we knew that God would not bring us this far to leave us on our own.

Almost a year and a half after, everything first happened; our numbers were back up. We were doing better than we thought possible. I believe that it was through the prayers and faith of my coworker and I that brought our small daycare through when other government funded daycares shut down for good. God blessed our little daycare with grants and funds that helped keep us afloat until things got better and started getting back to normal. God's timing is better than ours every time—even if we don't it during those challenging times.

> Therefore, God elevated him to the place of
> highest honor and gave him the name above all
> other names, that at the name of Jesus every knee
> should bow, in heaven and on earth and under
> the earth, and every tongue declare that Jesus

Christ is Lord, to the glory of God the Father.
(Philippians 2:9–11 NLT)

The New American Standard says verse 10 this way: "So that at the name of Jesus *every knee will bow*." Jesus has been given authority over every name. His name is above cancer, addiction, abuse, molestation, pain, loss, grief, suicide, illness, oppression, anything that can be named: Jesus is above it.

One of the most powerful stories in the Bible is found in Luke. There are actually two powerful stories woven together in this set of Scripture. Both, however, show off Jesus's power over two specific names: illness and death.

> On the other side of the lake the crowds welcomed Jesus, because they had been waiting for him. Then a man named Jairus, a leader of the local synagogue, came and fell at Jesus' feet, pleading with him to come home with him. His only daughter, who was about twelve years old, was dying. As Jesus went with him, he was surrounded by the crowds. A woman in the crowd had suffered for twelve years with constant bleeding, and she could find no cure. Coming up behind Jesus, she touched the fringe of his robe. Immediately, the bleeding stopped. "Who touched me?" Jesus asked. Everyone denied it, and Peter said, "Master, this whole crowd is pressing up against you. But Jesus said, "Someone deliberately touched me, for I felt healing power go out of me." When the woman realized that she could not stay hidden, she began to tremble and fell to her knees in front of him. The whole crowd heard her explain why she had touched him and that she had been immediately healed. "Daughter," he said to her, "your faith has made you well. Go in peace." While he was still speak-

ing to her, a messenger arrived from the home of Jairus, the leader of the synagogue. He told him, "Your daughter is dead. There's no use troubling the teacher now." But when Jesus heard what had happened, he said to Jairus, "Don't be afraid. Just have faith, and she will be healed. When they arrived at the house, Jesus wouldn't let anyone go in with him except Peter, John, James and the little girl's father and mother. The house was filled with people weeping and wailing, but he said "Stop the weeping! She isn't dead; she's only asleep." But the crowd laughed at him because they all knew she had died. Then Jesus took her by the hand and said in a loud voice, "My child, get up!" And at that moment her life returned and she immediately stood up! Then Jesus told them to give her something to eat. (Luke 8:40–55 NLT)

Mark 5:28 adds an important detail when it came to the woman with the issue of blood: "For she thought to herself, 'If I can *just touch* his robe, I *will* be healed'" (emphasis added). She believed she would be healed even if Jesus didn't say a word to her or even touched her ill body. I also love how Jesus finishes the conversation with the woman in verse 34: "And he said to her, 'Daughter, *your* faith has made you well. Go in peace. Your suffering is over.'" I don't know about you, but I would be bawling like a baby if I were in her shoes.

I want to explain a little more about this situation the woman was in and why it was so powerful.

If a woman has a flow of blood for many days that is unrelated to her menstrual period, or if the blood continues beyond the normal period, she is ceremonially unclean. As during her menstrual period, the woman will be unclean as long as the discharge continues. (Leviticus 15:25 NLT)

Jesus was walking with them at this time, but the people still lived by the law of Moses. This woman suffered for twelve years with a constant flow of blood. From what I have researched, the purpose of this scripture was not to punish the women for having a natural body event but for sanitary reasons. We are blessed to have products that help us through such things now.

The woman knew that going to Jesus while on her flow was dangerous. The society back then was none too kind to those seen as "unclean." She carried this label on her for many years, and I suppose she had enough and decided to do something about her situation. Sometimes it's when we've had enough that our faith is strong enough to fight back against the circumstances we're facing.

Notice as well where it says she touched the fringe of his robe. That's the bottom of His robe. With all the people crowding around Jesus, she had to fight her way through them in order to get her healing. This was one determined lady that was not taking no for an answer! She was most likely stepped on, kicked, shoved; but she wasn't about to let that stop her! This lady was on a mission.

The last thing I want to mention about her is how God gave her a new identity. All those years she wore the label of "unclean" had to have taken a toll on her. That label had to affect her view on herself at some point. Jesus changed that. When He addressed her, he did so by calling her "Daughter." He gave her a new identity. Not just whispering it so only she could hear it; he said it loud enough for the crowd to hear. He wanted them to know the change in her identity as well.

The reason that this particular story has such a special place in my heart is due to the fact that I had issues with irregular periods ever since I was young. It's a generational thing that has affected most, if not all, the women in my family. This woman's story was powerful; I felt like there was hope for me too. If Jesus could heal her, He could heal me.

So I prayed.

For years. I prayed for the same healing that this sister in Christ received. There were times I have doubted that it will happen, but I firmly believe it will. For now, I am thankful for the medical aid I am able to receive in order to manage this issue until my body is healed. There are times that I struggle with doubt because I wasn't seeing anything happening in the natural. There were times I wondered if God really heard me, or if healing was something He wanted for me.

I have to keep believing until my worldly, fleshly body aligns itself with God's words of healing. I speak the scriptures over myself. This woman's determination to get healed is an inspiration!

Don't grow weary if your healing or if your breakthrough is taking longer than you'd like. Hold firm to God and keep believing while you wait. I've heard it said that just because we don't see things in the natural world doesn't mean there aren't angels fighting for us in the supernatural to get us what we've asked for.

I believe the reason this woman's testimony was combined in the telling of Jairus and his family crisis was because both of these people had sought out Jesus specifically. The woman with the issue of blood sought him out with the thought that he could heal her. While we don't know Jairus's thoughts we do know that he got some unfavorable news before Jesus was able to make it to his home. Notice that Jairus doesn't grumble saying that the woman with the issue of blood had stopped them long enough that his daughter's death resulted in their delay. Jesus told him to just have faith.

Verse 50 states, "When Jesus heard this, he said 'Jairus, don't yield to your fear. Have faith in me and she will live again'" (The Passion Translation).

This news was a chance for Jairus to make a very important decision. He could choose to trust in Jesus and believe that regardless of the circumstances Jesus would come through, or he could allow the fear of losing his daughter to overcome him and suppress his faith in Jesus.

This lesson is important to understand: When circumstances of life come our way, we have a choice to make. Will we give into fear? Or will we press on in faith?

It's not always easy to press in. If anything it will go against what the world tells you to do, your physical body and your mind will fight you as well. Pressing into your faith will contradict what well-wishers around you say, what your doctor may say, maybe even what your spouse says. You have to believe that God's will for your life will happen. It probably won't be on your timeline, but God is never late. The choice in the end is yours. Which road will you take? Only one can take you into a deeper relationship with God.

8

Progress Is Growth

Identity is a vital part of who we are. What we believe about ourselves impacts our ability to connect with others as well as how we view ourselves and what we believe we can do with our life. Our identity could stem from those in our family, our friends, but painfully for many can identify themselves by the circumstances they have gone through in life that have knocked them down and left them at rock bottom.

Your identity, dear one, isn't given to you by others or by your circumstances. It is given to you by God. You can choose to accept labels that others attempt to place on you. Ultimately, it is God that defines you. Below are a few verses on how God views you. Take your time when reading them and allow these verses to penetrate any negative views you may have of yourself.

> *Yet look at you now! Everything is new!* Although you were once distant and far away from God, now you have been brought delightfully close to him through the sacred blood of Jesus-you have actually been united to Christ! Our reconciling "Peace" is in Jesus! He has made Jew and non-Jew one in Christ. By dying as our sacrifice, he has broken down every wall of prejudice that separated us *and has now made us equal*

through our union with Christ. (Ephesians 2:13–14 TPT, emphasis added)

And now, because we are united to Christ, we both have equal and direct access in the realm of the Holy Spirit to come before the Father! So you are not foreigners or guests, but rather *you are the children of the city of the holy ones, with all the rights as family members of the household of God. You are rising like the perfectly fitted stones of the temple,* and your lives are being built up together upon the ideal foundation laid by the apostles and prophets, and best of all, *you are connected to the Head Cornerstone of the building, the Anointed One, Jesus Christ himself!* This entire building is under construction and is continually growing under his supervision until it rises up completed as the holy temple of the Lord himself. This means that God is transforming each of you into the Holy of Holies, his dwelling place, through the power of the Holy Spirit living in you! (Ephesians 2:18–22 TPT, emphasis added)

You are a work in progress. That is not a bad thing! As I've mentioned before, you don't have to be perfect in order to make your way to the Father. He loves you and wants to help you grow into who He has created you to be.

Every story in the Bible shows a person who was learning who God created them to be. Even Jesus had to learn who He was and what God had planned for Him. There are other powerful verses when it comes to our old—before Christ—identity:

For since we are *permanently* grafted into him to experience a death like his, then we are *permanently grafted into him to experience a resurrection like his and the new life that it imparts.*

Could it be any clearer that our old former identity is now and forever deprived of its power? For we were co-crucified with him to dismantle the stronghold of sin within us, so that we would not continue to live one moment longer submitted to sin's power. (Romans 6:5 TPT, emphasis added)

So let it be the same way with you! Since you are now joined with him, you must continually view yourself as dead and unresponsive to sin's appeal while living daily for God's pleasure in union with Jesus, the Anointed one. Sin is a dethroned monarch; so you must no longer give it an opportunity to rule over your life, controlling how you live and compelling you to obey its desires and cravings. (Romans 6:11–12 TPT)

And you did not receive the "spirit of religious duty" leading you back into the fear of never being good enough. But you have received the "Spirit of full acceptance" enfolding you into the family of God. And you will never feel orphaned, for as he rises up within us, our spirit joins him in saying the words of tender affection, "Beloved Father!" For the Holy Spirit makes God's fatherhood real to us as he whispers into our innermost being, *"You are God's beloved child!"* (Romans 8:15–16 TPT, emphasis added)

What a powerful and beautiful scripture! We don't have to go back into the fear of not being good enough! How amazing is that once we grasp that fact! When I first read this scripture, it made me pause for a moment and realize that I didn't have to feel like I wasn't enough for God. My past, present, and even future mistakes didn't disqualify me from Him being able to use me. I pray the scripture gives you the same comfort and excitement for the future. You will never be too messed up for God to use you for His glory.

This was a great comfort as He put it on my heart to address one of the long-standing addictions in my life. For a long time, I attempted to take care of the symptoms of an issue. I hadn't realized that I hadn't addressed the root of the issue. I thought that my addictions to pornography and masturbation were the root issue, but recently, I discovered that they weren't. The addiction was a symptom. The issue, the root issue, was an issue with my identity.

For so long, I looked to others in my life—friends, church members, people I met online—to fill the void in my life. I looked to them to call me loved, worthy, special, needed, precious, wanted. That last one was a big one.

Coming from a broken family, I struggled with feeling unwanted and unfit in my family. My parents divorced when I was under the age of two. Society wasn't kind to those of us with "broken" families, and I relied too heavily on society for approval.

I never addressed this issue head-on because my biggest fear was that it would be confirmed by those I longed for acceptance from. I was terrified my family would say that I was unwanted and unfit to be a part of their family. I knew in my heart this wasn't true, but I struggled with the lie for many years.

The issue with my identity back when I was a child had effects on my life as I grew older. Back when I was in my late teens, I thought I'd be married with at least one kid by thirty. I grew jealous when I was in my twenties seeing others around my age getting married and having kids. That jealousy led to me being insecure in myself and my faith in God's timing.

Ever since I hit middle school, I'd struggled with my weight and self-esteem. I wasn't the popular girl, and getting a boyfriend was something that society said gave you value. If you didn't have a romantic relationship, then your worth was less than those that did. I know now that this is one of the biggest lies out there, but at the time, I didn't and that lead me to rushing God's timing.

When I broke up with my ex at twenty years old, I thought I was letting go of the only guy who would ever be interested in me. I thought I wouldn't find anyone else. It had taken a fight between us for me to realize how toxic the relationship was, and that for my own health, I needed to break things off. While I thought I was falling apart when the relationship ended, God was using it for His glory.

I was falling together even when I thought I was falling apart. I learned through that experience what I would be willing to put up with and what I wouldn't when it came to a relationship. I had learned there have to be boundaries and following through with those boundaries had to happen even if it meant dissolving the relationship. I thought I'd learned my lesson, but just a few years later, I met a young man that would change my life—and not for the better.

We had chatted on a now nonexistent social media site for a few months before agreeing to meet in person. At the time, I hadn't realized how desperate I was for validation, for someone to be interested in me for who I was. I still believed that if someone was interested in you, you had more value than if you were single.

At the time, I wasn't as close to the Holy Spirt as I should've been. I can still remember hearing that still small voice telling me, "No! Don't go!" when he invited me over to his house one evening. I didn't think anything of it; I was excited for the chance to be alone with him.

Now, there are times in our lives that we say, "If I could go back and change [situation from the past] I would!" Well, as much as I wish I could say that about this situation, I can't. That night, I ended up giving up my first—by choice—time with him. I ignored all those red flags that I'd seen. I ignored the lesson I thought I'd learned from my last relationship, and I ignored the still, small voice that warned me not to go. The Holy Spirit was trying to warn me to not to be led by my emotions.

The emotional pain that I went through after making that decision was something I wouldn't wish on anyone.

I learned that I never wanted to have sex before marriage with anyone again. It had been a mistake I couldn't take back. I had to work at accepting what I had done. I had major suicidal thoughts after my mistake with him. I wondered how God could forgive me for doing something I'd promised Him and myself that I would never do. I had wanted so badly to wait until I was married to be sexual with someone, but I ended up making that mistake because I wasn't feeding my faith as much as I was feeding my insecurity. I allowed myself to think that he was the only guy out there that was going to show any interest in me, and instead of praying about it, I settled.

After it happened, I was in so much emotional pain and I didn't know who to turn to, but I knew that I had to reach out to someone or I was going to end up doing something I regretted.

I ended up telling my stepsister about what happened, and she comforted me; she could tell just by looking at me something happened. When I opened up to another Christian friend of mine, however, I learned not all Christians are those you want to share certain issues with. This particular friend told me that essentially I had screwed up, so why wait any longer to do it with anyone else? This was the beginning of the end of that friendship.

As I processed what I had done, I begged God to take my feelings for him away if he wasn't the one for me. It took about two weeks for those feelings to fade away completely, but they did.

It took a long time for me to open up to anyone else about it after that experience, but as I have learned, I'm not the only one that's made that mistake. I've been able to be a comfort to someone who came to me making the same mistake many years later, and I was able to give her guidance in how to handle the emotional damage that came along with premarital sex.

The main thing I learned was this: Ladies: Do. Not. Pursue. That is the guy's job. If a guy is interested, he will make the effort to connect with you without compromising your values. This isn't to say you can let a guy know you're interested in him, but do not pursue a relationship. Know who you are in Christ and hold fast to *that* fact before even considering giving any guy your heart. Understand that your value has nothing to do with your marital status.

Identity is the center of who we are. If we don't know who we are, how do we stand against the storms of life? A failed relationship will begin to feel like it's defining you. Broken friendships will make you question your worth. Broken family due to divorce or loss of a parent can cripple your identity if that's where your identity was located.

We can't rely on things from this world to give us our identity. Remember, we were told *not* to be conformed to this world. We can't build our lives on anything that will crumble and fall when the storms of life come. We have to put our identity, our foundation on solid ground. Jesus is that solid ground. I am well aware just how much easier this is said than done. I've been through situations where a storm took away a good friendship, and I had to readjust where my footing was located. It's not an easy thing to do, but if you set your foundation on Christ early on, it will save you pain later on down the road.

> Everyone who hears my teaching and applies it to his life can be compared to a wise man who built his house on an *unshakeable* foundation. When the rains fell and the flood came, with fierce winds beating upon his house, it stood firm because of its strong foundation. But everyone who hears my teaching and does not apply it to his life can be compared to a foolish man who built his house on sand. When it rained and rained and the flood came, with wind and waves beating upon his house, it collapsed and was swept away. (Matthew 7:24–27 TPT, emphasis added)

For a time, I was like the foolish man building my identity on the opinion of those around me. I based my identity on if anyone was interested in me romantically or not. I based my identity on what my friends thought of me. This led to a major struggle in high school between my faith and my friends. I tried to draw closer to Christ, but I also wanted to be the person I thought my friends wanted me to be.

This is part of what led to my addiction. In a fantasy world, I could become whoever I wanted. I could be the creator and have things go how I wanted them to go. If a character I created had to go through drama, I controlled how much it affected her, if those relationships stayed or went away. This was an attempt at some type of control in a difficult time, a grasp for control over the issues in my life I had no control over. I tried to run away to something imaginary in order to ignore the pain in real life instead of addressing it head-on. This wasn't healthy and led to years of pain later on down the road.

God opened my eyes during a worship night at my church. I was sitting on the floor, and I told God I wanted to let go of my addiction to fantasy, which included inappropriate role plays and stories online. I didn't want to hold onto that muck and hold onto His hand at the same time. I knew I needed to let it go. It was while I was sitting on the floor during that worship night that I began to take notes for this book. I wrote the following:

- Addiction to fantasy
- Looking for acceptance
- Looking for connection
- Feeling lack of purpose/visibility
- Lack of identity → wanting to be someone "better"
- Self-worth issues

> I lost my identity when I was molested. I didn't know who I was, I identified as my sin, felt lost, looked to fantasy to fill the void; didn't see myself as anything other than broken and not good enough.

9/29/21

> Worship night broke down the wall. I am worthy because of Jesus. I am exactly as God created me to be: "Creative, smart, love children." Mentor prayed with me; felt the walls breaking down.

> I will no longer put my worth in the hands
> of others. My worth comes from Jesus *alone!*

During that night, a friend and mentor came over to pray with me and said that Satan doesn't care who he hurts. He doesn't care if he hurts or kills babies, children, innocents; none of that matters to him. What matters is getting what he wants, and he will do anything in his power to do so.

She said there was a reason Satan attacked me at such a young age through molestation, addiction, and suicidal thoughts. He wanted to stop me from fulfilling the plans and purposes God has for my life. He wanted to stop this book from being written. He wanted to stop the impact I would have on the children in my school as a teacher and the children in my life. He didn't win. He didn't win, and he won't in the future. He will lose, and Jesus will win. No matter what tricks he tries he is living on borrowed time.

We have to find our identity in Christ. There is no other choice. Everything else that this world has to offer will fail us every single time we attempt to rely on it as it's just temporary and not eternal. Christ won't. Jesus is there with us through it all, even when we feel like we're going through the fire alone He is right there with us.

> Shadrach, Meshach, and Abednego replied, "O Nebuchadnezzar, we do not need to defend ourselves before you. If we are thrown into the blazing furnace, the God whom we serve is able to save us. He will rescue us from your power, Your Majesty. But *even if he doesn't,* we want to make it clear to you, Your Majesty, that *we will never serve your gods or worship the gold statue you have set up.*" Nebuchadnezzar was so furious with Shadrach, Meshack, and Abednego that his face became distorted with rage. He commanded that the furnace be heated seven times hotter than usual. Then he ordered some of the strongest men of his army to bind Shadrach, Meshach, and

Abednego and throw them into the blazing furnace. So they tied them up and threw them into the furnace, fully dressed in their pants, turbans, robes, and other garments. And because the king, in his anger, had demanded such a hot fire in the furnace, the flames killed the soldiers as they threw the three men in. So Shadrach, Meshach, and Abednego, securely tied, fell into the roaring flames. But suddenly, Nebuchadnezzar jumped up in amazement and exclaimed to his advisers, "Didn't we tie up three men and throw them into the furnace?" "Yes, Your Majesty, we certainly did." they replied. "Look!" Nebuchadnezzar shouted. "I see four men, unbound, walking around in the fire unharmed! And the fourth looks like a god!" Then Nebuchadnezzar came as close as he could to the door of the flaming furnace and shouted: "Shadrach, Meshach, and Abednego, servants of the Most High God, come out! Come here!" So Shadrach, Meshach, and Abednego stepped out of the fire. Then the high officers, officials, governors, and advisers crowded around them and saw that the fire had not touched them. Not a hair on their heads was singed, and their clothing was not scorched. They didn't even smell of smoke! Then Nebuchadnezzar said, "Praise to the God of Shadrach, Meshach, and Abednego! He sent his angel to rescue his servants who trust in him. They defied the king's command and were willing to die rather than serve or worship any god except their own God. Therefore, I make this decree: If any people, whatever their race or nation or language, speak a word against the God of Shadrach, Meshach, and Abednego, they will be torn limb from limb, and their houses will be turned into heaps of rubble. There is no other

god who can rescue like this!" (Daniel 3:16–28
NLT, emphasis added)

There will be times in our lives when God will not keep us from going through hard times. He uses those hard times to strengthen our walk with Him. Our reliance, our dependence on Him is strengthened in times of trouble. Shadrach, Meshach, and Abednego faced death for defying the king; but their faith and identity in God was so strong they were willing to do what God called them to do fully knowing that in doing so it could result in their death.

From my research, the three were close to Daniel, and Daniel faced his own death threats for worshiping God against a king's order. He was thrown into the lion's den, but God shut the mouths of the lions, and Daniel was spared.

In the difficulties of life, we have two choices: Trust God or don't. While we may not know *why* we go through certain hardships in life, that doesn't mean that God isn't faithful *in* them.

There was a saying I read some time ago that struck me deeply: If we have all the facts, we trust in them more than we trust in God. Ouch. How often have you wanted to know the facts *before* you'd be willing to trust God? I'll admit, I've done it before many times. I've wanted to see the end result in order to make my own suggestions to God's plan before we go through with it. That's not how it works, though. God knows the plans and purposes He has for us; we have to trust that fact regardless of how impossible things may seem He will be faithful through it all.

> And we know that God causes everything
> to work together for the good of those who love
> God and are called according to his purpose for
> them. (Romans 8:28 NLT)

There was a time when I was struggling with viewing myself as God saw me; I was still in the midst of my addiction and was trying to understand *how* God could see me as something special when I couldn't see it. My friend challenged me to write down how God viewed me using Scripture. I looked up Scriptures online and wrote down a list, and from there, I wrote out each and every scripture on a piece of paper. Most of the scriptures I found I had already read before, but I didn't think they included me as I thought my mistakes were too big for God to forgive.

> Do not copy the behavior and customs of this world, but let God transform you into a new person by changing the way you think. Then you will learn to know God's will for you, which is good and pleasing and perfect. (Romans 12:2 NLT)

> And I am certain that God, who began the good work within you, will continue his work until it is finally finished on the day when Christ Jesus returns. (Philippians 1:6 NLT)

> For we are God's masterpiece. He has created us anew in Christ Jesus, so we can do the good things he planned for us long ago. (Ephesians 2:10 NLT)

There were scriptures I had heard growing up and going to church that I didn't think applied to me. I knew God loved me, but I didn't understand how He could forgive me for everything that I'd done, the struggles that I dealt with for years felt like they were winning, and I wondered if God really saw me this way.

I didn't believe that God saw me as precious. What was so special about me? I wasn't thin or popular. I wasn't on a sports team in high school. I didn't even have an outgoing personality. I didn't believe I was qualified for God to think that way about me. I thought I had to earn that view from Him.

I thought there was something wrong with me, that God couldn't use me if I wasn't an outspoken, energetic type of person. What could God do with an overweight, glasses-wearing bookworm that had a hard time getting her thoughts together? For those of you with ADD or ADHD, you understand the struggle.

> You are altogether beautiful my darling;
> there is no flaw in you. (Song of Songs 4:7 NIV)

I had heard people talk about how some verses just *spoke* to them, but I had never truly understood what they meant. Until I read that scripture. It felt like everything around me was put on pause. My thoughts, which were normally buzzing around like a bee on an energy drink, were stilled for the first time in my life.

Altogether…*all together*…every bit of what made me who I was and am. All of it. God didn't say "Altogether…except your weight, or thin hair, or the red specks on your arms and legs that you hate so much [or insert your personal insecurity here]." No. All of me. All of *you*. God saw me as beautiful, and He sees you as beautiful too!

He doesn't see my flaws as I do. That love for books? He gave it to me. That plush body I wished was thinner, He doesn't see me as fat. The plush I hated so much growing up is often what the children in my life cuddle up to when they need comfort. I am able to be a safe place for them. What we sometimes wish to be rid of is something God put in us for a specific reason.

God calls me "darling." He calls *you* "darling." He has pet names for us! He loves us. It's difficult to understand as we may not love ourselves, but He loves us. He loves you. You don't have to look like whatever celebrity is *in* now. I spoke of this verse before, but it's a good reminder:

> But the LORD told him, "Samuel, don't think Eliab is the one just because he's tall and handsome. He isn't the one I've chosen. People judge others by what they look like, but I judge people by what is in their hearts." (1 Samuel 16:7 CEV)

I wish most teens would read and understand this scripture when it comes to dating. That's for another book, though!

People of this world will accept or reject you based on your appearance, your accomplishments, the amount of money you have in your bank, the size of your house or car, the label on your clothes. This is a fact of life. God doesn't.

Robert Burns said it well when he said, "I would rather stand with God and be judged by the world than stand with the world and be judged by God. Thank you, Jesus Lord of my life."

Our identity will change over time for many reasons. A job change, a marriage or the loss of it, becoming a parent, an aunt, an uncle, caring for an elderly parent, or accomplishing a lifelong goal.

The foundation of our identity needs to be in Christ Jesus. Everything else about ourselves is subject to change due to the seasons of life. This is something that is inevitable for every person alive. Like a ship in the storm, God is our anchor if we find our identity in Him and Him alone. It takes time to do this, but don't give up. You won't regret throwing away the world's view in favor of God's view of you.

9

Who Has Your Focus?

Some time later, the Lord spoke to Abram in a vision and said to him, "Do not be afraid, Abram, for I will protect you, and your reward will be great." But Abram replied, "O Sovereign Lord, what good are all your blessings when I don't even have a son? Since you've given me no children. Eliezer of Damascus, a servant in my household, will inherit all my wealth. You have given me no descendants of my own, so one of my servants will be my heir." Then the Lord said to him, "No, your servant will not be your heir, for you will have a son of your own who will be your heir." Then the Lord took Abram outside and said to him. "Look up into the sky and count the stars if you can. That's how many descendants you will have!" And Abram believed the Lord, and the Lord counted him as righteous because of his faith.

—Genesis 15:1–6 (NLT)

Any time you read about someone in the Bible, aside from Jesus, there will be a moment where they point out their situation or circumstances to God. With Abraham, he pointed out to God that he had no son. With Moses, he pointed out that he stuttered. With Gideon, he pointed out his position in his family. Even with Mary, the mother of Jesus, she pointed out her situation of being a virgin.

We think with our rational and earthly mind, while God's thoughts are on another level than our own. This is one of the reasons why we must put our faith in Him and believe that His plans are going to come to pass in His timing, even if we have no understanding *how* it will happen.

There will be times where our choices, our mistakes, may seem to take us off the path that God has for us. Sarah, Abraham's wife, struggled with believing that God would truly give her a child. In this time of doubt, she encouraged Abraham to have a child with one of her servants. This mistake didn't stop God from fulfilling His promise to Abraham.

> Then God said to Abraham, "Regarding Sarai, your wife-her name will no longer be Sarai. From now on her name will be Sarah. And I will bless her and give you a son from her! Yes, I will bless her richly, and she will become the mother of many nations. Kings of nations will be among her descendants." Then Abraham bowed down to the ground, but he laughed to himself in disbelief. "How could I become a father at the age of 100?" He thought. "And how can Sarah have a baby when she is ninety years old?" So Abraham said to God, "May Ishmael live under your special blessing!" But God replied, "No-Sarah, your wife, will give birth to a son for you. You will name him Isaac, and I will confirm my covenant with him and his descendants as an everlasting covenant." (Genesis 17:15–19 NLT)

In this Scripture, we see Abraham once again looking at his circumstances. This time, his focus is on his old age. Instead of trusting in God, doing as He said He would, Abraham looked at his physical limitations. This is a cycle we can get stuck in ourselves if we're not careful. If God says He's going to do something, we'd best believe it even if we can't see the end result. God will fulfill His promises to us.

There will be times when we go through moments of doubt. Even if we end up off track, God can still bring us back and fulfill the plans and purposes He has for our life. We just have to be willing to repent, forgive ourselves, learn from those mistakes, and use it to push us forward stronger than before. Allow God to use those times to propel you forward and not allow them to hold you back from what God has called you to do.

There are times I've looked at my past and wondered how God could use something as messed up as what I've got to offer. I've tried to hide those things from God and make it seem as if they never happened, but it never worked. While the things I have gone through in life haven't always been easy or joyful, they do have a purpose. All through the writing of this book, God has been reminding me that my past may connect with someone who ends up with this book. This book may give them the hope to keep going even when all they see around them is darkness, loneliness, hopelessness, or loss. The things we go through lose their power to condemn us when we allow God to use them for His glory.

> The Lord kept his word and did for Sarah exactly what he had promised. She became pregnant, and she gave birth to a son for Abraham in his old age. This happened at just the time God had said it would. And Abraham named their son Isaac. Eight days after Isaac was born, Abraham circumcised him as God had commanded. Abraham was 100 years old when Isaac was born. And Sarah declared, "God has brought me laughter. All who hear about this will laugh with me. Who would have said to Abraham that Sarah would nurse a baby? Yet I have given Abraham a son in his old age!" (Genesis 21:1–7 NLT)

God blessed Abraham and Sarah with a child even when they went through times of doubt. He does the same for us. We don't have to be perfect in order to be blessed by God. We don't have to jump through hoops for God to love us. Abraham showed his faithfulness to God in a later chapter when he was willing to sacrifice Isaac.

Some time later, God tested Abraham's faith. "Abraham!" God called. "Yes," he replied. "Here I am." "Take your son, your only son-yes Isaac, whom you love so much- and go to the land of Moriah. Go and sacrifice him as a burnt offering on one of the mountains, which I will show you." The next morning Abraham got up early. He saddled his donkey and took two of his servants with him, along with his son Isaac. Then he chopped wood for a fire for a burnt offering and set out for the place God had told him about. One the third day of their journey, Abraham looked up and saw the place in the distance. "Stay here with the donkey." Abraham told the servants. "The boy and I will travel a little father. We will worship there, and then we will come right back." So Abraham placed the wood for the burnt offering on Isaac's shoulders, while he himself carried the fire and the knife. As the two of them walked on together Isaac turned to Abraham and said "Father?" "Yes, my son?" Abraham replied. "We have the fire and the wood, "The boy said. "But where is the sheep for the burnt offering?" "God will provide a sheep for the burnt offering, my son." Abraham answered. And both walked on together. When they arrived at the place where God had told him to go, Abraham built an alter and arranged the wood on it. Then he tied his son, Isaac, and laid him on the alter on top of the wood. And Abraham picked up the knife to kill his son as a sacrifice. At that moment the angel of the Lord called to him from heaven, "Abraham! Abraham!" "Yes," Abraham replied. "Here I am!" "Don't lay a hand on the boy!" The angel said. "Do not hurt him in any way, for now I know that you truly fear God. You have not withheld

from me even your son, your only son." Then
Abraham looked up and saw a ram caught by its
horns in a thicket. So he took the ram and sac-
rificed it as a burnt offering in place of his son.
(Genesis 22:1–13 NLT)

There are quite a few things that happen in this section of scripture! It's incredible that Abraham was so willing to sacrifice his only
son to show God that he was faithful. I want to point out a few
things that he did in this situation.

First off, notice how when he was speaking to the servants, he
didn't say, "I will come right back." He said, "We will come right
back." He knew that one way or another, God was either going to
bring his son back to life, or he wasn't going to have to sacrifice Isaac
after all. His faith in God was shown even before he made his way up
the mountain with his son.

Secondly, when Isaac asked where the lamb was for the sacrifice
Abraham was quick to point out that God would provide what they
needed. I'm sure this was not only to reassure himself of the promise
God had made to him but to reassure his son as well.

Is there something in your life that you need to be willing to sacrifice to prove to yourself that you love God? This is done to remind
ourselves that God needs to be the center of our life. We need to
prove to ourselves that God is more important than whatever it is in
our life that may be special to us or something we're praying for to
come to pass in the future.

God has to come first.

Not your husband nor your boyfriend. Not your children, not
your job, your possessions, not even your church. God has to be first
in your life.

This doesn't mean that you don't value those things, but you
don't look to them to fulfill the desires of your heart. You don't look
to those things for strength to overcome hardships.

God is asking for our focus, your attention be on Him first.
That we put our faith, our hope, our trust in Him and Him alone.

Focusing our attention on God looks different for each person. Some people can sit and read the Bible for hours on end while others can listen to worship music and praise God without growing weary of doing so. Some are called to spend hours in a closet praying in tongues.

I don't believe there is any "right" way to glorify and praise God. Each of us has a unique way of doing so that feels most natural for us. Ask God to guide you when it comes to dedicating your time to Him. Just as we each receive love in different ways, we can express our love to God in different ways as well.

I struggled for a long time with guilt for not spending hours reading my Bible or sitting and praying for an hour in the morning before work. I didn't think that listening to worship music on my way to work counted as spending time with God. While those other methods are important, it's also important to know what's the best way for *you* to show your love to God. We can train ourselves in other ways—reading, worshiping, praying—but there's one way that feels natural. Practice that natural way daily, but work on practicing the others as well.

I read a book that spoke of love languages and how they relate to how we love God. One of the chapters spoke of a wife that spent time reading her Bible and could get lost in doing so while her husband would find himself lost in worship during church. The two of them had different ways to love and honor God, and one wasn't right over the other. Find what way works best for you to worship and dedicate your time with God.

Abraham wasn't the only person that had his moments of doubt and his focus on the wrong thing. Moses also had quite the history behind him when God called on him to bring His people out of Egypt.

> Many years later, when Moses had grown up, he went out to visit his own people, the Hebrews, and he saw how hard they were forced to work. During his visit he saw an Egyptian beating one of his fellow Hebrews. After looking

> in all directions to make sure no one was watch-
> ing, Moses killed the Egyptian and hid his body
> in the sand. The next day, when Moses went out
> to visit his people again, he saw two Hebrew men
> fighting. "Why are you beating up your friend?"
> Moses said to the one who had started the fight.
> The man replied, "Who appointed you to be our
> prince and judge? Are you going to kill me as you
> killed the Egyptian yesterday?" Then Moses was
> afraid, thinking, "Everyone knows what I did."
> (Exodus 2:11–14 NLT)

Moses made a decision he regretted the next day not because he knew that what he'd done was wrong, but because he was afraid of other people knowing. In our day and age, this would be considered killing in defense of another, but that didn't apply back in those days. It was an eye-for-an-eye kind of culture. Due to people knowing about what Moses had done, he had to flee, leaving his home, ending up in Midian where he married and had children.

It was years later that God called on him when he was tending to his father-in-law's sheep.

> "Now go, for I am sending you to Pharaoh.
> You must lead my people Israel out of Egypt." But
> Moses protested to God, "Who am I to appear
> before Pharaoh? Who am I to lead the people of
> Israel out of Egypt?" God answered, "I will be
> with you. And this is your sign that I am the one
> who has sent you: When you have brought the
> people out of Egypt, you will worship God at this
> very mountain." But Moses protested, "If I go to
> the people of Israel and tell them, 'The God of
> your ancestors has sent me to you,' They will ask
> me, 'What is his name' Then what should I tell
> them?" God replied to Moses, "I AM WHO I
> AM. Say this to the people of Israel: I Am has

sent me to you." God also said to Moses, "Say this to the people of Israel: Yahweh, the God of your ancestors-The God of Abraham, the God of Isaac, and the God of Jacob- has sent me to you. This is my eternal name, my name to remember for all generations." (Exodus 3:10–15 NLT)

But Moses protested again, "What if they won't believe me or listen to me? What if they say, 'The LORD never appeared to you'?" (Exodus 4:1 NLT)

But Moses pleaded with the LORD, "O Lord, I'm not very good with words. I never have been, and I'm not now, even though you have spoken to me. I get tongue-tied and my words get tangled." Then the LORD asked Moses, "Who makes a person's mouth? Who decides whether people speak or do not speak, hear or do not hear, see or do not see? Is it not I, the LORD? Now go! I will instruct you in what to say. But Moses again pleaded, "Lord, please send anyone else." (Exodus 4:10–13 NLT)

Moses fought God's calling on him to the point that God agreed to let Aaron, his brother, join him on the journey. God agreed to use both Moses and Aaron to speak to the Pharaoh and save His people. How often do we question God or come up with excuses?

When God calls us to do something in life, are you the type of person that jumps on board right away, ready to go, full of faith and willing to do whatever God needs to be done? Or do you act more like Moses? Do you have questions, doubts, do you try to get God to choose someone else because they may be better qualified for what God wants to do compared to yourself?

There is a reason God chose to use you for a specific mission. He knows your faults. He knows where you're lacking, but it is because

He knows these things that He chose you. When we rely on Him to do the things He has called us to do, we draw ourselves closer to Him for guidance and help. If we believe that we're overqualified for what God's called us to do, we tend to believe that we can do it better on our own, by our own abilities, our own might, our own power instead of relying on God. We can fall into pride if we see what God has called us to do as beneath our abilities.

If God calls you to do it—whether it be picking up trash in your church's parking lot, working with the homeless, raising children, or running a multimillion-dollar company—remember who you are doing it for. You're not doing it for yourself, but you're doing it to honor God. If you don't see it that way, maybe you need to take a step back and reevaluate where your focus and attention lies.

> If you keep quiet at a time like this, deliverance and relief for the Jews will arise from some other place, but you and your relatives will die. Who knows if perhaps you were made queen for just such a time as this? (Esther 4:14 NLT)

More often than not, you will be called out of your comfort zone. This is where growth happens. When we're comfortable, it's easy to become complacent and forget that we're supposed to be striving, growing, working to become better. Comfortable and familiar are not always what's best for us. Before we're saved, sin is comfortable.

> Stay alert! Watch out for your great enemy, the devil. He prowls around like a roaring lion, looking for someone to devour. (1 Peter 5:8 NLT)

It's important to remember that the enemy is looking for any weak spots we may have so he can pounce on them and drag us away from God. If we're striving to draw closer to God, then we don't give him—the devil—a chance to catch us unaware.

There will be times in life where you will be thrown into the deep end, with no preparation, no warning. It is during times like these that your foundation is tested. As some say, this is where you find out if you sink or swim.

Esther was an orphan. Her cousin had adopted her into his family and was one of many women taken to King Xerxes when his first queen had disobeyed him, and in his anger, he had banished her from the kingdom. If you are unfamiliar with the story, King Xerxes was throwing a party (one that lasted seven days!) and requested that the queen make an appearance. She refused. Some say this was because she did not wish to be paraded around; others say that the request was for her to appear wearing just her crown on her head. Whatever the request was, the queen refused. As a result, she was banished.

After the king had calmed down and realized the mistake he had made in his anger, his attendants suggested that he find a new queen to take her place. It doesn't say how the women were selected, but Esther was one those chosen. Before she left Mordecai informed her not to disclose the information of her family to anyone. This was most likely due to the fact that Jews were in the minority where they lived. Esther found favor with the king and was chosen to become queen in Vashti's place.

It doesn't say how long Esther was a queen before Haman began his plot against Mordecai. He, Mordecai, begged Esther to go to the king knowing she was the only one that could convince him to save them as Haman planned to have the Jews killed for living differently than the rest of the realm. Knowing she faced possibly faced death either way, Esther fasted and prayed before bringing herself before the king, knowing fully well that she could be killed by appearing to him without being requested. When the king accepted her presence, she didn't speak her request outright, no; she asked him to join her for a banquet. It was during the second banquet she requested he join her at that she made her request known to him:

> So the king and Haman went to Queen
> Esther's banquet. On this second occasion, while
> they were drinking wine, the king again said to
> Esther. "Tell me what you want, Queen Esther.

What is your request? I will give it to you, even if it is half of the kingdom!" Queen Esther replied, "If I have found favor with the king, and if it pleases the king to grant my request, I ask that my life and the lives of my people will be spared. For my people and I have been sold to those who would kill, slaughter, and annihilate us. If we have merely been sold as slaves, I could remain quiet, for that would be too trivial a matter to warrant disturbing the king." "Who would do such a thing?" King Xerxes demanded. "Who would be so presumptuous as to touch you?" Esther replied, "This wicked Haman is our adversary and our enemy." Haman grew pale with fright before the king and queen. Then the king jumped to his feet in a rage and went out into the palace garden. Haman, however, stayed behind to plead for his life with Queen Esther, for he knew that the king intended to kill him. In despair he fell on the couch where Queen Esther was reclining, just as the king was returning from the palace garden. The king exclaimed, "Will he even assault the queen right here in the palace, before my very eyes?" And as soon as the king spoke, his attendants covered Haman's face, signaling his doom. (Esther 7:1–8 NLT)

After Haman was taken away, the king made a decree that allowed the Jews to protect themselves against those that wished to kill them. The king wasn't the one that created the decree, however. He gave that responsibility to Mordecai. Esther and Mordecai were put in a situation that seemed hopeless, but Esther overcame through the power of God. She prayed, she fasted, and she faced death for her people. She overcame by the power of God.

I want to take a moment to talk about the former queen.

I believe that God made Queen Vashti with a good heart and a stubborn streak. (Most of us women have this streak as well.) I believe that in Queen Vashti's disobedience to the king, God opened a door for Esther to be made queen and, in turn, protect her people from the plot Haman had made due to her uncle's "disrespect" to him. I'm sure at the time no one could have guessed that God was working the queen's banishment for His people's ultimate good by saving them from death.

There will be situations in your life where you may need to do as Esther did and pray and fast. It's imperative to our faith to feed our faith and not our fears. Even when the situation you are facing seems like it's a mountain, that's when it's imperative to press into God even more.

God is bigger than that mountain you're facing. He is bigger than your circumstance. He is bigger than your situation. If you allow Him, He, too, can use what was meant to harm you, to hinder you, to prevent you from moving forward, to propel you forward farther than you even thought was possible.

10

Truth Shall Set You Free

You have placed our wickedness before you, Our
secret sins [which we tried to conceal, You have
placed] in the [revealing] light of Your presence.
—Psalm 90:8 (AMP)

I don't know about you, but this verse even made me cringe a bit. So
often in our lives, we think that we can conceal our sin. Perhaps we
can from other people, but we can't from God. He knows everything
we've done and will ever do. While that can be terrifying I want it to
give you a sense of hope. Scriptures like this used to scare me; they
would make me think that if God knew everything I would do, He
could decide that I wasn't doing enough, that I wasn't fighting against
my addiction enough, that I was too much hassle and just leave me
be. I was terrified of God abandoning me because He saw my sins.

This verse, while it does make me cringe, it also gives me hope.
Nothing we do is new to God. He already knew that we screwed up
and that we will continue to screw up. He knew that we looked at
pornography last week, that we cheated on a test back in the fifth
grade, that we fell in our recovery of our addiction, that we lied to
our parents about where we'd been when we were out, all of it. He
already knows.

The fact that He already knows gives hope because He knows,
and He hasn't left us. He hasn't abandoned us to figure it out on our
own. He hasn't said to us, "You've had five years to figure out the

right path to take, and you're not listening so you're on your own." No, He is still right there beside us, holding out His hand to us with nothing but compassion and love in His eyes for us.

There are many reasons why someone may fall into an addiction, but regardless of the reason they started, there is always hope. There is always a way out. No matter if you've been addicted for a week, a month, three years, or fifteen years. There is hope. There is help. The only thing you can't do is give up on yourself.

Earlier, I shared about my struggle with addiction to pornography. When most people think of addiction, they think of things that can be harmful: drugs, alcohol, pornography, medication. But addiction isn't limited to just that area. There are those that are addicted to praise from others in their lives; some are addicted to pleasing others. Other people are addicted to social media (seriously, though, I think most of us are). There are people addicted to food or shopping. There's no limit to things that people can be addicted to; it's not always a substance issue.

I've spoken about many people's stories throughout this book. When I was preparing to write this chapter, I asked a close friend if she'd be willing to discuss her addiction with me and how God has brought her through it. I mentioned Shannon, Jenn, and myself having addictions in our lives as well; but Samantha was kind enough to talk specifically on addiction and how she's on the road to recovery.

In the year 2020, she was going through some stressful events in her life. "I remember the day that I got addicted to gasoline. I was pumping my car at AARCO, and I was under a lot of stress. I had just lost my job as a cleaning person. I said to myself, *I don't want to do any other drugs.* I didn't want to pop pills or shoot up with needles so I said, 'Hey! I'll just take a whiff of this,' and that was the biggest mistake of my life."

That's a phrase heard quite often by those dealing with or recovered from addiction. The choice to give into the temptation just once can spiral into something they can't control any longer.

"The more stress I felt, the more I wanted to sniff. I liked the feeling of it. I liked how it numbed my mind and took me away from what was really happening."

I resonated with her on this in my own way. The escapism that addiction first promises. "If you give in once, you'll feel better," and you give in and tell yourself that you won't fall into it again, that once was enough, but then, the trigger (in her case as well as my own: stress) gets hit again, and that temptation is back with another "You'll feel better." It can quickly spiral out of control.

Escapism never helps the issue that we're facing, though. It doesn't make the situation go away; it just gives you an excuse to not deal with it during that time. Addiction makes the situation worse over time as we chose to ignore it in favor of our addiction.

"What lead me to stop was it went from doing it once in a while to doing it four or five times a day and hiding it from those I cared about. I never brought it into the house because I was afraid of what my friend might say or think, and I knew I had to quit, but I couldn't. After losing my niece to a sudden accident, the addiction got worse. What really stopped me from doing it was seeing the news about another woman dying at fifty-three years old. She had been addicted to gasoline since she was thirteen. The day I found out she died, I took my last whiff." At the time this interview was taken, Samantha was five months clean. She made it to one year in August of 2022 and is still fighting the good fight.

One of the enemy's favorite tactics is to tempt us then condemn us. He will entice us to fall into doing something we know is wrong, especially when we have a history of being addicted, and then shame us when we do fall into that temptation. His goal is to keep us silent about our struggles with others. When we try to fight the battle of addiction on our own, we are bound to fail. God created us to have relationships, and relationships are what help pull us out of the muck and gunk that addiction covers us in.

When asked how she felt after opening up about her addiction, Samantha responded, "I feel like a huge weight is off my back. Ever since I told my friend about my addiction, I feel like I'm 100 lbs. lighter. Seeing the woman die the way she did, I said, 'Whoah, I have to stop. I have to stop now.'" Sometimes it takes a real shock of reality for us to realize just how deep we're in and how much we need help. Bringing light to the addiction you're struggling with is the best way to begin your path to healing. Don't allow it to hide in the darkness a moment longer.

Addiction doesn't define you. At the same time, addiction does not have limits. It will continue to take from you until there's nothing left to take. The devil will fight you when it comes to bringing your addiction to light and sharing your experience with others. He will make you think that you're alone, that you're broken, that no one will understand you, that no one will look at you the same way again if you tell them what you've been through—or in some cases, *are* going through.

He is the father of lies. I have to be honest here: there will be some who will reject you because of your history, but there will be others who will be inspired by your strength to not only recognize your addiction but address it. The strength to overcome addiction doesn't come by way of our own flesh and spirit; it comes through the Holy Spirit, from God. It's when we realize that we can't do it on our own that we throw up our hands in surrender and ask God to help us; that is when God can move in our lives and help lift us up out of the gunk even when we've walked into that gunk willingly.

> Consider it nothing but joy, my brothers and sisters, whenever you fall into various trials. Be assured that the testing of your faith [through experience] produces endurance [leading to spiritual maturity, and inner peace]. (James 1:2–3 AMP)

When it comes to breaking free of addiction, this advice was given by Samantha: "The best way to start is to recognize that you have a problem. And you have to be willing to admit to yourself that you have a problem before you admit to someone else. You have to be willing to give up that addiction for everything. Addiction is giving up everything for that one thing, but recovery is giving up that one thing for everything." At some point in your journey, you have to decide which is more important to you, your addiction or God. The moment you turn away from your addiction and turn to God, He will meet you where you are.

There are those that are freed from their addiction right away while others, it takes time for their freedom to become a reality. Even if you stumble on the road to recovery, you've got to pick yourself back up and keep on moving forward. You can't give up when things get difficult. That's when it's most important to have godly relationships around you that will pick you up and help you continue on the path toward God.

Relationships are vital when it comes to every area of our life, especially when fighting an addiction. If we try to battle it by our own power, on our own, we will surely fail because we are human and can only do so much alone. When support surrounds you, and you cling to God tighter than you cling to your addiction, every day you will draw closer and closer to your freedom. Each day that chain will become a little weaker until one day it breaks off. God wants you to be free. Only He can truly set you free.

Freedom from addiction is possible, and God using our addiction for His glory is possible. While life would be easier if we didn't have to carry these things on our shoulders, I believe that in going through these experiences, we are able to not only help others who need it, but it draws a deeper dependence on God as well. You never know how amazing it could feel to know that someone else has been in the same storm you're in, and they tell you how God brought them through it.

Through the experience of addiction, we can realize just how much we need God in our lives to help us through our weakest areas. This type of dependence on God is not a bad thing. God *wants* us to be dependent on Him not because He needs to feel needed or appreciated or loved. He needs us to be dependent on Him because *that* is when He is able to really get to work in our lives. He created us. He knows us better than we know ourselves. The moment we step out of the way and allow Him control He is able to do more for us than we could ever ask or think.

Be prepared to go to war. After being freed from her addiction to gas, the enemy attempted to hit Samantha in another area of her life.

We have to fight. Make the choice to fight every day against the attack of the enemy. With God on your side, you can't lose!

One of the hardest parts about dealing with addiction—be it drugs, alcohol, sex, porn, or even something like anger or jealousy—was finding resources that can help you.

When I realized I needed to address my addiction to porn and masturbation, I knew that I needed help; I just didn't know where to start. When I looked online, 99 percent of what I found was targeted toward men. This didn't help me as the reasons for my addictions were different from the reasons men often turn to porn.

There were times this made me feel even more isolated; that something was wrong with me for being a female and struggling with a mostly male problem. Condemnation was another large factor that affected my attempt to reach out for help. The way that some people wrote about those struggling with addiction only added fuel to the fire of condemnation I was struggling with. While they meant well, they treated the pornography addiction as if it was leprosy and made someone untouchable. It didn't offer the hope that one could be freed from such sins.

As a survivor of childhood sexual abuse, these almost cookie-cutter type of articles only helped in making me feel that I was alone. That I could never overcome my past. That I was useless to God unless I could overcome this sin on my own.

First John 3:8 and scriptures like it for some time terrified me as I didn't understand the context fully when I was younger.

> The one who does what is sinful is of the
> devil, because the devil has been sinning from the
> beginning. The reason the Son of God appeared
> was to destroy the devil's work. (NIV)

You can imagine why scriptures like this terrified me! I had thought for the longest time that God hated me because I sinned. I was too young to consent to sex before marriage, but in my mind, not saying no and not fighting it meant I consented. I took what I read at face value and didn't understand the underlying context or the culture. I didn't even understand God's grace back then. These scriptures scared me when I struggled with viewing porn as well. I didn't want to, but I couldn't get enough of it at the same time. I was disgusted by my addiction, but I was also addicted to the point I felt there was no hope.

Praise God He's given me a deeper understanding of this scripture in another version: "But when people keep on sinning, it shows that they belong to the devil, who has been sinning since the beginning" (NLT).

The devil can twist this scripture to fit what he wants it to say. He can use it to increase the condemnation we feel. I'm not saying that we have freedom to sin. I'm saying that sin is a part of our life. We need to fight it, but we will never be truly 100 percent sinless until we get to heaven. That's why we need Jesus.

The Amplified says it even better:

> The one who practices sin [separating himself from God, and offending Him by acts of disobedience, indifference, or rebellion] is one of the devil [and takes his inner character and moral values from him, not God]; for the devil has sinned and violated God's law from the beginning. The Son of God appeared for this purpose, to destroy the works of the devil.

It continues in verse 9:

> No one who is born of God [deliberately, knowingly and habitually] practices sin. Because God's seed [His principle of life, the essence of His righteous character] remains [permanently] in him [who is born again-spiritually transformed, renewed, and set apart for His purpose]; and he [who is born again] cannot habitually [live a life

characterized by] sin, because he is born of God
and longs to please Him.

Even now, while writing this scripture out for you, I feel renewed! How amazing our God is! He doesn't expect us to be perfect. He doesn't expect us to live a sinless life as I mentioned before. If that were possible, why send Jesus to die for us? Reading this scripture in this version renewed my hope. It helped me understand the deeper layers to it that one version didn't. I'm not saying that you should disregard that first version I shared. What I'm saying is, if you are unsure what a specific verse or set of verses may mean, then there is no shame in looking to other versions for clarification.

If after doing this you're still not clear, try praying to God for clarification or reaching out to a *trusted* friend or mentor for some help. There is no shame in not knowing something; it's okay to reach out and ask for help.

One thing I struggled with understanding was this "habitual" sin. I thought all sin was wrong, and it is. What I didn't understand was the flesh versus the spirit fight. When we are born again, our spirit is renewed—that is what goes to heaven.

The flesh is our physical bodies. Our physical bodies are not reborn. Our souls are not reborn either; our soul is where our mind, will, and emotions reside. This is where free will comes in.

Our flesh (body) and spirit are at constant odds with each other. The flesh wants to draw closer to worldly things while our spirit wants to draw closer to the things of God. Our soul is where we make the decision to either follow our flesh or follow our spirit. We can draw closer to righteousness and God or sin and death.

This is why we as Christians still struggle every single day with sin. This explains why we sometimes fall into sin. The thing is we don't have to do is stay there when we do fall.

The difference between habitually sinning and falling into sin is this: When you habitually sin, you are not trying to fight it. You don't see your sin as something bad, harmful, a hindrance to your relationship with God and others, and therefore, you don't fight against it.

Essentially, you've given up trying to win the fight against the sin in your life and chose to live a sinful life regardless of the consequences.

There is hope for those living in habitual sin. You can choose to change. You can invite Jesus into your heart and ask him to help you change, to help that desire to live in that sin to die off, and he will help you. It may take time, but the relationship we can have with God is worth more than all the pleasure sin can offer us. God's love is eternal while the pleasure of sin will forever be temporary.

On the flipside, when you fall into sin, it's normally because you've tripped up. I would fall into sin when I hadn't been reading my Bible as much as I should have and was allowing myself to indulge in more flesh-focused activities: TV shows I shouldn't be watching, stories I shouldn't be reading, etc. Unlike habitual sin, though, you don't stay down when you fall and accept defeat. When you do fall into sin, you pick yourself back up, dust yourself off, and get back on the spiritual road walking with God. You keep getting back up to fight the good fight of faith no matter how many times you fall.

This trip up may happen daily, weekly, monthly, or perhaps yearly. You keep fighting, though! No matter how many times you fall, you don't throw your hands up and give up trying. You persevere even when it seems like you're only making baby steps on your journey.

Those baby steps begin to add up over time. That choice to get back up and dust yourself off strengthens you each time you get up again. I will warn you; there will be people that will say that you are not saved because you have sin in your life. Often, these types of people take scripture out of context and are unwilling to look at themselves and their own shortcomings.

They can use scriptures similar to the ones below:

> Therefore you are to be *perfect*, as your heavenly Father is perfect. (Matthew 5:48 NLT, emphasis added)

> For we all stumble in many ways. And if anyone does not stumble in what he says, he is

a *perfect* man, able also to bridle his whole body. (James 3:2 ESV)

To these scriptures, I respond the following:

> Not that I have already *obtained* it or have *already become* perfect, but I press on so that I may lay hold of that for which also I was laid hold of by Christ Jesus. (Philippians 3:12 NASB, emphasis added)

> Indeed, we *all* make many mistakes. For *if* we could control our tongues, we would be perfect and could also control ourselves in every other way. (James 3:2 NLT, emphasis added)

> And He has said to me, "My grace is *sufficient* for you, for power is perfected in *weakness*." Most gladly, therefore, I will rather boast about my *weakness*, so that the power of Christ may dwell in me. (2 Corinthians 2:19 NASB)

God is the standard, not man. Which is why we need Jesus as we can't make it through this life alone. There is nothing we can do in our own power that could ever save us from the sin and death that reign in this world. We know—because Jesus has showed us—what's right and wrong, and when we fight, we're strengthened not because of what *we* can do but because of what *He* is doing *in* us!

> If we say we have no sin, we deceive ourselves and the truth is not in us. (1 John 1:8 NASB)

> You, therefore, will be perfect [growing in spiritual maturity both in mind and character, actively integrating godly values into your daily

life], as your heavenly Father is perfect. (Matthew 5:48 AMP)

All of us who are mature [pursuing spiritual perfection] should have this attitude. And if in any respect you have a different attitude, that too God will make clear to you. (Philippians 3:15 AMP)

Let's go back to see what "attitude" we should have:

Not that I have already obtained it [this goal of being Christlike] or have already been made perfect, but I actively press on so that may take hold of that [perfection] for which Christ Jesus took hold of me and made me His own. Brothers and sisters, I do not consider that I have made it my own get; but one thing I do: forgetting what lies behind and reaching forward to what lies ahead. I press on toward the goal to win the [heavenly] prize of the upward call of God in Christ Jesus. (Philippians 3:12–14 AMP)

Jesus made you His own. You don't have to allow sin to control your life any longer. Keep pressing into Him, and each day will get a little easier. There will be tough days, and there will be storms of life, but they are more bearable when we have Jesus as the foundation under our feet.

This Christian life we live, it won't always be sunshine and rainbows. That is why it is vitally important to be sure that we are maturing in our faith. We do this by attending church, reading books that help us gain a deeper understanding of who God is, having mentors that can lift us up to the next level. This isn't a complete list, but it's a start.

I'm obviously not trying to flatter you or water down my message to be popular with men, but my supreme passion is to please God. For if all I attempt to do is to please people, I would not be the true servant of the Messiah. (Galatians 1:10 TPT)

And then our immaturity will end! And we will not be easily shaken by trouble, nor led astray by novel teachings or by the false doctrines of deceivers who teach clever lies. But instead we will remain strong and always sincere in our love as we express the truth. All our direction and ministries will flow from Christ and lead us deeper into him, the anointed Head of his body, the church. (Ephesians 4:14–15 TPT)

Growth, maturity, whichever you prefer to call it, is our choice. No one can force us to decide to grow deeper into God's Word, but if we want to overcome the situations this life will throw at us, that is exactly what we must do. We are at war even if we don't realize it. The enemy is trying anything and everything he can to stop us from reaching out with the Word of God to those who need to hear it.

I recall relying on the faith of others when I was first starting out, and that's okay! It's not where we are supposed to stay, however. Your testimony will be able to reach someone else that needs to know that God is for them and not against them. In order to do that, you must prepare yourself to fight so you're equipped to help those around you prepare to fight as well. God is with us and will never leave us nor forsake us.

As I stated before, there will be times when it seems like you're speaking to a mountain and it's not moving. It will seem like what you're doing, what you're praying for, speaking the word for, won't come to pass. You may think that you're doing something wrong, that you've missed a memo, or that you simply aren't "Christian" enough. You can't give up. Jesus spoke of how important it is for the ground a seed is to be grown on to be soft, ready soil.

> The seed that fell on the beaten path represents the heart of the one who hears the message of the kingdom realm but doesn't understand it. The Adversary then comes and snatches away what was sown into his heart. The seed sown on gravel represents the person who gladly hears the kingdom message, but his experience remains shallow. Shortly after he hears it, trouble and persecutions come before the kingdom message he received. Then he quickly falls away, for the truth didn't sink deeply into his heart. The seed sown among weeds represents the person who receives the message, but all of life's busy distractions, his divided heart, and his ambition for wealth result in suffocating the kingdom message and preventing him from bearing spiritual fruit. As for the seed that fell upon good, rich soil, it represents the hearts of people who hear and fully embrace the message of heaven's kingdom realm. Their lives bear good fruit-some yield a harvest of thirty, sixty, even one hundred times as much as was sown." (Mathew 13:19–23 TPT)

There will be times in your life when you may experience one or more of these types of grounds in your life. When I was first starting off as a Christian back in middle school, I dealt with my path being the beaten path. I didn't understand how God could love me, how Jesus could forgive me for everything I'd done, and what I was struggling with. I was set free from the condemnation of the sexual abuse, but I was still mentally struggling with figuring out who I was and understanding who God really was.

In my high school years, I matured to gravel ground. I still attended church, but my understanding of God still wasn't there. I would fall back into old habits and try to fight them off with my own power, but if I fell often enough I struggled with wondering if I'd ever truly be free. This continued into college where I matured to having ground with weeds.

My focus on finding my identity left me struggling to feel accepted and loved. This resulted in making a mistake that I couldn't take back, and that's when things started to change for me. That was the breaking point where I knew I had to change something in my life. At the time this happened, my niece was around two or three years old. I wanted to be a good example to her as well and knew that in order to do so, I had to change something about the road I was on.

I can say now that my ground is good and rich. I have to give credit where credit is due, and I wouldn't be where I am today without my church and the relationships I've established through it.

The support and love from my church has been what has brought me through some of the hardest storms the last five years. I thought the storms I went through *before* I drew closer to God were tough. They may have been, but had I been hit with the storms I've faced back then I know for sure I would've been washed away. My foundation wasn't strong back then.

It's never too late for you to decide to make God the center of your life.

God loves you and accepts you where you are, but He doesn't want you to stay there. He wants to use you and your story for His glory.

Even when you fall, get back up and keep on fighting the good fight of faith.

11

Your Unique Path

Then Jesus said, "Come to me, all of you who are weary
and carry heaven burdens, and I will give you rest. Take my
yoke upon you. Let me teach you, because I am humble and
gentle at heart, and you will find rest for your souls. For my
yoke is easy to bear, and the burden I give you is light."

—Matthew 11:28–30 (NLT)

It doesn't always feel like the truth, does it? The burdens we sometimes carry on our shoulders can seem to crush us under them. Did
you ever think that perhaps that is because it's not our burden to
carry?

If we carry a burden of self-esteem issues, Jesus wants to take
that. He wants you to see yourself as He sees you—a precious child,
fully loved by God.

And I will be your Father, and you will be
my sons and daughters, says the Lord Almighty.
(2 Corinthians 6:18 NLT)

But to all who believed him and accepted
him, he gave the right to become children of
God. They are reborn-not with a physical birth
resulting from human passion or plan, but a birth
that comes from God. (John 1:12–13 NLT)

> For all who are lead by the Spirit of God are children of God. So you have not received a spirit that makes you fearful slaves. Instead, you received God's Spirit when he adopted you as his own children. Now we call him, "Abba, Father." For his Spirit joins with our spirit to affirm that we are God's children. (Romans 8:14–16 NLT)

One of the most important things when it comes to being children of God is that we don't have to walk through this life alone. No matter what our family life looks like, no matter our relationship status, or even how many friends we have, we can walk alongside Jesus in this life; and with His help, we can overcome those situations that the enemy meant to destroy us.

There may be a situation in your life where you don't know how you'll come through on the other side, but God will provide a way if you trust in Him. Some would call this "blind faith" but the Bible is accessible, and your faith in God is not blind. His glory is shown to us through our daily life. All you have to do is look at the intricacies in the human body to see God's amazing work.

There will be those in your life that will not understand or agree with the way you're living your life when you run after God. My pastor talks openly about his history, and he spoke of how before he was saved, his family hadn't said a thing about the road he was going down as they were on the same one, but the moment he got saved and decided to go to Bible school, they all had something to say about it—none of it supportive.

It's difficult when those you care about don't support what you're doing; sometimes they don't understand it because they don't live with the same hope that you do. Jesus is our hope and our guidance when things get difficult. At times, you will have to make a choice: Who do you want to please more? Your spouse, your boyfriend, your family, your friends? Or God? The choice is ultimately up to you.

And David danced before the Lord with all his might, wearing a priestly garment. 2 Samuel 6:14 NLT)

David was willing to make a fool of himself dancing before God. He was a king, but his faith, his relationship with God was more important than how other people viewed him. He held strong to his decision even when his wife criticized him.

When David returned home to bless his own family, Michal, the daughter of Saul, came out to meet him. She said in disgust, "How distinguished the king of Israel looked today, shamelessly exposing himself to the servant girls like any vulgar person might do!" David retorted to Michal, "I was dancing before the Lord, who chose me above your father and all his family! He anointed me as the leader of Israel, the people of the Lord, so I celebrate before the Lord. Yes, and I am willing to look even more foolish than this, even to be humiliated in my own eyes! But those servant girls you mentioned will indeed think I am distinguished!" (2 Samuel 6:20–22 NLT)

There will be times in our lives where what we're doing may seem foolish to those around us, but if God has called us to do something, then we need to do it even if the world calls us names for following what God is guiding us to do. David wasn't the only person who was willing to make himself look like a fool to those around him.

Noah had to deal with months, possibly even years of condemnation, taunting, and mockery for not only himself but his family as well. He was determined, however, to honor God. Not only did Noah have to stand against what society considered "normal," but he then had to have faith that God would bring him through a trial no one else would ever experience.

For forty days the floodwaters grew deeper, covering the ground and lifting the boat higher above the earth. As the waters rose higher and higher above the ground, the boat floated safely on the surface. Finally, the waters covered even the highest mountains on the earth, rising more than twenty-two feet above the highest peaks. All the living things on earth died-birds domestic animals, wild animals, small animals that scurry along the ground, and all the people. Everything that breathed and lived on dry land died. God wiped out every living thing on the earth-people livestock, small animals that scurry along the ground, and the birds of the sky. All were destroyed. The only people who survived were Noah and those with him in the boat. And the floodwaters covered the earth for 150 days. But God remembered Noah and all the wild animals and livestock with him in the boat. He sent a wind to blow across the earth, and the floodwaters began to recede. The underground waters stopped flowing and the torrential rains from the sky were stopped. So the floodwaters gradually receded from the earth. After 150 days, exactly five months from the time the flood began, the boat came to rest on the mountains of Ararat. Two and a half months later as the waters continued to go down, other mountain peaks became visible. After another forty days, Noah opened the window he had made in the boat and released a raven. The bird flew back and forth until the floodwaters on the earth had dried up. He also released a dove to see if the water had receded and it could find dry ground. But the dove could find no place to land because the water still covered the ground. So it returned to the boat, and Noah held out his hand and drew the dove back inside. After waiting another seven days, Noah released the dove again. This time the dove returned to him in the evening with a fresh olive leaf in its beak. Then Noah knew that the floodwaters were almost gone. He waited another seven days and then released the dove again. This time it did not come back. Noah was now 601 years old. On the first day of the new year, ten and a half months after the flood began, the floodwaters had almost dried up from the earth. Noah lifted back the covering of the boat and saw that the surface of the ground was drying. Two more months went by and at least the earth was dry! (Genesis 7:9–8:14 NLT)

Noah had to hold out faith that God wouldn't allow the boat to float on forever. He had to be patient and trust in the Lord during this time where he couldn't go anywhere. I could only imagine how difficult that time must've been for him. Noah showed that at times you have to hold onto the faith that God hadn't forsaken you when you've been stuck on a boat for a year or sometimes longer.

Noah and David were just two examples of men that followed the calling that God put on their lives. They were ridiculed by those around them, but they were faithful in following the path God guided them down. There are times we may be called to go down a similar path they did. They put their faith in God, and it's vitally important we do the same.

There is a calling God has put on your life. No two people are the same, and no two people have the exact same calling. They may share similar callings, and in such, they can support each other when things get difficult. Each person has their own circle of people that they can impact, which includes those they may interact with while pursuing the calling God has put on their lives.

> Only, let each one live the life which the Lord has assigned him, and to which God has called him [for each person is unique and is accountable for his choices and conduct, let him walk in this way]. This is the rule I make in all the churches. (1 Corinthians 7:17 AMP).

I used to feel like I was less than others around me when it came to the calling on my life. For some time, I didn't even *know* what my calling was. When I did find my passion, I struggled with seeing my calling as valuable. This was due to my viewing my calling not being as glamorous as other people's callings were. Being a teacher isn't a job that pays well; it isn't a job that was or is recognized as important by most of society. Often, this job can give very little but expects abundantly more in every way possible: mentally, emotionally, and especially physically.

For a long time, I would see people being called into the ministry, being called into going overseas and building churches, healing people, running large businesses; and I would think, *I'm just a teacher. I just work with these little children. How am I making a difference in the world? How am I supposed to help the people hurting in this world if I'm barely able to make ends meet myself? My job isn't as important as my sister who's a nurse.*

These types of thoughts would kill my passion to pursue my calling from God. I would wonder if God made a mistake, if I'd missed something that resulted in me being stuck in a job where I had little benefits, little pay for my expected higher education, continued education, and little recognition. This was heavy on my heart for a long time, and I began to wonder if I should just walk away from this and find a job that may not be a passion but would at least pay me enough to take care of myself.

It was during a worship night that God opened my eyes and poured out on my spirit that I was doing exactly what He created me to do. He put a passion for children in my life. He put a passion for seeing them learn, cheering them on as they grew older and moved on to elementary school. He put a passion that would flare up every time I was around a child. There was something there, and I think kids could see it too. I'd have random kids I didn't know from Adam staring at me at restaurants in the store, just living my life. It was like they could recognize what I hadn't about myself. There was a spark there that they noticed, but I'd chosen to ignore or thought it was an insignificant spark compared to someone else's.

During that worship night, I took the time to appreciate that God put the desire to work with children in my heart. I acknowledged that it doesn't pay the best, but God provided for me regardless. I was reminded how I was able to rent an apartment from my family and had enough left over to put aside a savings account as minor as it was it was still money I could put aside. I wasn't recognized for what I did by society, but the parents often told me about the impact I had on their child's life and how much it meant to them to know their children enjoyed school, or how they appreciated having someone love on their child while they were away at work.

After working in the childcare field for over half of my life, I realize just how difficult this calling is. It's not for the faint of heart. God gave me this calling for a reason: Because He knew I could do it with Him by my side.

> Whatever you do [whatever your task may be], work from the soul [that is, put in your very best effort], as [something done] for the Lord and not for men, knowing [with all certainty] that it is from the Lord [not from men] that you will receive the inheritance which is your [greatest] reward. It is the Lord Christ whom you [actually] serve. (Colossians 3:23–24 AMP)

I had a close friend at the time tell me during that worship night that I was showing Jesus to those kids by my actions. I couldn't preach to them because they wouldn't understand what I was talking about—my class age being one- to almost-three-year-olds—but I could walk in love as I worked with them. I could show them how to walk in the love that Jesus walked in. I could teach them compassion.

I could lead by example. It can be one of the best ways to teach others because they can't argue your actions like they can your words.

Nothing warmed my heart more than when I had a kiddo upset over something that had happened and two or three other children coming over—without instruction from me—and rubbing that child's back or giving them a hug or a toy. Moments like that made me want to cry as I was so proud of the love these sweet children carried in their hearts. There was a reason Jesus told his disciples not to deny the children from coming to him.

> Seeing what was happening, Jesus called for the parents, the children, and his disciples to come and listen to him. Then he told them, "Never hinder a child from coming to me but let them all come, for God's kingdom belongs to them as much as it does to anyone else. These children demonstrate to you what faith is all about. (Luke 18:16 TPT)

While your calling might not have you recognized by the world, it is a calling God made especially for you. There is something that God included when He created you that would draw you to this particular passion. It could be a passion for people it could be a passion for art or a passion for words. Allow God to guide you in how He wants you to use that passion in your life. Use that passion to honor God and to show the world how faithful, how beautiful, how loving God is.

It doesn't matter how many times you have messed up in your life. It doesn't matter if you've run as far away from that calling as possible. It doesn't matter if you locked that calling up and refused to recognize it. It's there. If you allow God to help you utilize it, you'll be able to do more for the kingdom of God than you ever anticipated. All you have to do is trust, ask, and believe that God will help you.

As I wrote earlier in the book, it can become so easy to compare ourselves to others in one way or another. Sometimes we compare our callings to others, as I did. There are endless ways we can find to compare what we find wrong or different about ourselves to traits we see in others as right or better.

This is especially true when the world's current society values one profession, attribute, or trait, one quality more than another. While they praise firefighters, business professionals, and nurses, they condemn police, teachers, garbage workers, and fast-food workers.

If anything was shown during the shutdown of our country in 2020, it showed that it's those underappreciated jobs that keep this country going. There is no shame in being in the working class. There's no shame in not having a college degree. There's no shame in doing a job that keeps the world going. Trade workers are needed just as much as those with degrees.

Teachers worked hard to provide for their students to learn even when they were unable to be in the classroom, school bus drivers worked to deliver food to those students in need, nurses worked longer hours with higher patient numbers, the police worked hard to protect those that need help. You notice when the garbage man misses your garbage one week. When the weather gets bad, those that work the snow plows put themselves in harm's way to clear the roads.

My point is this: Many jobs or callings seem as if they're not as glamorous as others. It can be so easy to find ourselves in comparison to those with those "glamorous" jobs. Before I was secure in my calling to work with kids, I often compared myself with my younger sister. She knew before high school that she wanted to be a nurse. She took the medical classes offered at the high school starting as a freshman and went on to go to two different colleges away from home to get her bachelor's in nursing.

I've shared about my story throughout this book, and I mentioned before about my issues with thoughts of suicide. It wasn't just about the addiction that would lead me to those thoughts. I had mental issues, lies I believed for years, that lead me to comparing myself to my own family.

During this time, the book of Romans was one that had a few nuggets that helped give me strength to make it through. These verses began to plant little seeds in my heart that took root and kept me from ending my life.

There were two specific times I felt the spirit of God physically touch me when I was on the brink of suicide. Both of these times, I struggled with seeing my value, understanding God's love and forgiveness, and feeling like I belonged. I didn't know or understand my calling. I thought I had to have it all figured out and that everyone else already had a playbook for their life, that I was the odd one out.

The first time I was holding a knife in my hand, thinking how easy it would be for me to slice my wrist and just let go. As I was thinking this, I felt a hand on the back of mine, and I heard the softest voice say, "Don't." When I heard this voice, my heart felt as if it was being enveloped in love, and I put the knife down and tried to understand what it was that just happened. I knew God was real and He loved me, but this was the first time I heard His voice.

The second time, I was in the bathroom holding a bottle of pills. I was thinking how easy it would be to just take them and go to sleep, never wake up again. This time, I felt that hand on mine again, the one holding the bottles, and instead of hearing a whisper, I felt warm arms wrapping around me and just holding me. It was almost to the point I couldn't even move, and I just broke down and cried on the bathroom floor. I knew it was God; I didn't understand how or why, but I knew it was Him, so I allowed myself to be comforted by Him.

> This righteousness of God comes through faith in Jesus Christ for all those [Jew or Gentile] who believe [and trust in Him and acknowledge Him as God's Son]. There is no distinction, since all have sinned and continually fall short of the glory of God, and are being justified [declared free of the guilt of sin, made acceptable to God, and granted eternal life] as a gift by His [precious, undeserved] grace, through the redemption [the payment for our sin] which is [provided] in Christ Jesus, whom God displayed publicly [before the eyes of the world] as a [life-giving] sacrifice of atonement and reconciliation (propitiation) by

His blood [to be received] through faith. This was to demonstrate His righteousness [which demands punishment for sin], because in His forbearance [His deliberate restraint] He passed over the sins previously committed [before Jesus's crucifixion]. (Romans 3:22–25 AMP)

When we were utterly helpless, Christ came at just the right time and died for us sinners. Now, most people would not be willing to die for an upright person, though someone might perhaps be willing to die for a person who is especially good. But God showed his great love for us by sending Christ to die for us while we were still sinners. And since we have been made right in God's sight by the blood of Christ, he will certainly save us from God's condemnation. For since our friendship with God was restored by the death of his Son while we were still his enemies, we will certainly be saved through the life of his Son. Now we can rejoice in our wonderful new relationship with God because our Lord Jesus Christ has made us friends of God. (Romans 5:6–11 NLT)

So the trouble is not with the law, for it is spiritual and good. The trouble is with me, for I am all too human, a slave to sin. I don't really understand myself, for I want to do what is right, but I don't do it. Instead, I do what I hate. But if I know that what I am doing is wrong, this shows that I agree that the law is good. So I am not the one doing wrong; it is sin living in me that does it. And I know that nothing good lives in me, that is, in my sinful nature. I want to do what is right, but I can't. I want to do what is good, but

I don't. I don't want to do what is wrong, but I do it anyway. But if I do what I don't want to do, I am not really the one doing wrong; it is sin living me in me that does it. I have discovered this principle of life—that when I want to do what is wrong, I inevitably do what is wrong. I love God's law with all my heart. But there is another power within me that is at war with my mind. This power makes me a slave to the sin that is still within me. Oh, what a miserable person I am! Who will free me from this life that is dominated by sin and death? Thank God! The answer is in Jesus Christ our Lord. So you see how it is: In my mind I want to obey God's law, but because of my sinful nature I am a slave to sin. (Romans 7:14–25 NLT)

That last scripture surprised me when I read it, but at the same time, I felt relief that I wasn't alone in my struggle. I wasn't the only one that loved God with every bit of who I was and still fell into sin.

Thank God, I'm not where I used to be. I'm not where I want to be yet, but I'm not where I once was, and that is an improvement! The fact that we're working, striving to get better and get closer to God is a sign that we're on the right path. Our salvation is meant to help draw us closer to God and farther away from sin. The closer you get to God, the less that sin will look appealing to you. Remember Romans 12?

Don't copy the behavior and customs of this world, but let God transform you into a new person by changing the way you think. Then you will learn to know God's will for you, which is good and pleasing and perfect. Because of the privilege and authority God has given me, I give each of you this warning: Don't think you are better than you really are. Be honest in your evaluation of yourselves, measuring yourselves by the faith God has given us. Just as our bodies have many parts and each part has a special function, so it is with Christ's body. We are many parts of one body, and we all belong to each other. (Romans 12:2–5 NLT)

In his grace, God has given us different gifts for doing certain things well. So if God has given you the ability to prophesy, speak out with as much faith as God has given you. If your gift is serving others, serve them well. If you are a teacher, teach well. If your gift is to encourage others, be encouraging. If it's giving, give generously. If God has given you leadership ability, take the responsibility seriously. And if you have a gift for showing kindness to others, do it gladly. Don't just pretend to love others. Really love them. Hate what is wrong. Hold tightly to what is good. Love each other with genuine affection and take delight in honoring each other. Never be lazy, but work hard and serve the Lord enthusiastically. Rejoice in our confident hope. Be patient in trouble and keep on praying. When God's people are in need, be ready to help them. Always be eager to practice hospitality. Bless those who persecute you. Don't curse them; pray that God will bless them. Be happy with those who are happy and weep with those who weep. Live in harmony with each other. Don't be too proud and enjoy the company of ordinary people. And do not think you know it all! (Romans 12:6–16 NLT)

Some people are called to be nurses, praise God! We need nurses! Some people are called to be teachers. Praise God! Some love working in the dirt and don't mind coming home smelling like something the cat dragged in. Praise God we need people who are willing to do what others don't appreciate until it's gone!

We need mothers, we need fathers, we need students, we need those who work with their hands, we need those who thrive in the sciences and know math that would make other people's heads spin.

Don't downplay your calling just because someone else has a "better" job than you. Be humble in what you do, and do it as if you're working for God. Do it with passion; do it with love! Shine your light regardless of where you may be at this moment in time. I can promise you one thing: You won't be there forever. That goes for the CEOs and those flipping burgers to get by.

We go through seasons of growth, and it's important to know that regardless of the season you are in, God will provide for you. It can be difficult in seasons where guidance may not be as clear as you want it to be, but it's during those seasons that we have a choice. We can choose to grow during those seasons, to press closer to God and rely on Him; or we can complain, gripe, and whine about where we're at and how we're not where we want to be.

The caterpillar doesn't go into the cocoon and becomes a butterfly overnight. It takes ten to fourteen days to become a butterfly, and there are some that don't even hatch until winter is over. If we're not careful, we can begin to compare our winter-long season to others' ten- to fourteen-day seasons. It can be so easy to complain about why we don't have what we want, but I believe that God does not hold back on us. It may not be our time, and He knows what He's doing. Sometimes we want things on our timeline instead of trusting in His timeline. Trust in His plan and His timing.

There are mistakes we make in life that if we changed them would change who we are today. Those mistakes aren't always fun; what should mistakes be? You do learn through those lessons if you allow God to teach you. You can use them to become stronger, to choose to go down a different path. It's never too late for God to use you even if you've made plenty of mistakes that would cause others to disqualify you from God's calling.

God loves you. He wants to mend your brokenness and turn those fractured pieces of your story into something beautiful.
Be patient in His timing.
Trust that He is with you
Be ready to be amazed by His work in you and through you.

> To all who mourn in Israel,
> he will give a crown of beauty for ashes,
> a joyous blessing instead of mourning,
> festive praise instead of despair.
> In their righteousness, they will be like great oaks
> that the LORD has planted for his own glory.
> (Isaiah 61:3 NLT)

Allow God to take those broken pieces. You won't be disappointed by what He does with them.

References

Amplified Bible. 2015. Lockman. https://www.biblegateway.com.

Contemporary English Version Bible. 1995. American Bible Society. https://www.biblegateway.com/.

English Standard Version Bible. 2001. Crossway. https://www.biblegateway.com.

New American Standard Bible. 1960. Lockman. https://www.biblegateway.com.

New International Version Bible. 1973. Biblica. https://www.biblegateway.com.

New Living Translation Bible. 1996. Tyndale. https://www.biblegateway.com.

The Passion Translation Bible. 2017. Broadstreet. https://www.thepassiontranslation.com/.

About the Author

Natasha Gray was born and raised in the Pacific Northwest. Her hobbies include crafting, reading, and photography. She attained her associate's in early childhood education from Clark College in 2013 and also earned her master's degree in theology from Faith Christian College in 2020. She is single and a first-time author and is pleased to share the words that had been put on her heart when she was but a spiritually lost child.

www.ingramcontent.com/pod-product-compliance
Lightning Source LLC
Chambersburg PA
CBHW031632170726
47990CB00017B/462